all in her head

all in her head

a novel

sunny mera

SHE WRITES PRESS

Published 2015

ISBN: 978-1-63152-818-7
Library of Congress Control Number: 2015942901

For information, address:
She Writes Press
1563 Solano Ave #546
Berkeley, CA 94707

She Writes Press is a division of SparkPoint Studio, LLC.

This book is dedicated to my loved ones, especially my daughter, whose gift of life brought me the opportunity to learn about my inner world. I wish you all the light from hope and love to guide you through any darkness you may encounter.

Author's Note

In 2005, ideas that can't have been true formed in my memory bank. After I had enough of these episodes to convince my family and doctors alike that I was suffering from more than the baby blues, I was diagnosed with postpartum delusional disorder, then psychosis in 2006. At first I underwent five months of treatment, then five years of treatment, then more treatment, until finally, in 2014, I changed providers and my diagnosis was reclassified as schizophrenia. Until they discover the cause of brain disease, I'll need treatment for the rest of my life.

In 2006, when I departed from the world as others know it for the first time and entered the world of psychosis, I experienced something I didn't know was possible. I had no exposure or reference to what psychosis was like, except for that movie *A Beautiful Mind*. My family had no awareness, and there was very little literature at the time available to me to understand my experience. When I came back from psychosis, it was soul-crushing to learn how drastically I had misunderstood my circumstances in my delusional state of mind. Still, those vivid memories remained a part of me, and I couldn't free myself from them. So I decided to write a story. I made the book fiction, because everyone who loves me told me when I was sick that I was delusional, and that my stories weren't real. They can't have been real, can they?

Introduction

I was born in 1977 and raised in a small, cottage-style home in a cultish community in Topeka, Kansas. I often played in the front yard with my big sister, Chloe, and my little brother, Erik. When I lifted the bricks that circled the strawberries around the lamppost, I'd watch the roly-polies uncurl and march along the surface until they found safety beneath the edge of the neighboring bricks.

My parents and their friends had a tight-knit community that shaped our minds as we grew up and gave me all kinds of knowledge about religion and classical literature for delusional memories to spring from. They loved learning and sharing about the works of the Inklings, an Oxford literary group of which C. S. Lewis, J. R. R. Tolkien, Francis Schaeffer, Charles Williams, and others were members. My parents' fascination with these authors inspired many of their own ambitions. Their reading list included *The Lord of the Rings*, *The Hideous Strengths*, *The Four Loves*, *The Great Divide*, *The Chronicles of Narnia*, and many more.

My parents met their friends during a campus crusade in 1970 at the University of Kansas and joined the K Group—"K" being short for "koinonea," meaning "friends." During their gatherings, they talked about their hopes and dreams for their future—the greatest of which was to start a school, based on a classical education that included their deeply spiritual Christian beliefs, where they could raise their children the way they wished they themselves had been raised. The core K Group met twice a week and continued to grow its vision for years; it incubated during the wives' pregnancies and gestated during the group's professional-degree programs.

In 1979 they chose to buy homes near each other in the Westboro neighborhood of Topeka. The small, cottage-style houses were within a few blocks of one another on a string of lanes and courts saddling two small parks. It was an intentional community with religious overtones.

The brand of Christianity I grew up with did not allow any objects to be glorified. There were no crosses on the walls, no Virgin Mary figurines, no votive candles or shrines, no saints or Jesus figures. There was only the Bible, and the Bible was the only word of God. I had a pink Precious Moments Bible that my parents gave me for Christmas when I was seven years old, with my name embossed on the cover in silver Times New Roman font.

My parents liked to go to church, although they believed that congregation and fellowship are anywhere you are and didn't feel you had to physically attend church to fulfill the requirement for worship. However, Sunday mornings were a great day for all of us. We'd wake up, and the glory routine would begin. Chloe and I would search through our wardrobe and pick out the perfect Sunday dresses, and Erik would put on a little suit that made him look like a miniature man.

Our education was intertwined with our religion. After the private Christian academy's formation in our attic, the founding fathers found a church over on Twenty-First Street to host Chloe's kindergarten class. My mom drove Chloe and me to school every day past the strip malls and shopping center on the main roads. Then she turned into the residential neighborhood and sped up a steep hill to get to that church. When I was in first grade, the school moved to its current location, on Clay Street in Topeka, and took the name Cair Paravel, after the castle in *The Chronicles of Narnia* where Queen Susan the Gentle, King Edmund the Just, Queen Lucy the Valiant, and High King Peter the Magnificent once ruled.

Our mothers sat talking for hours while all of us kids roamed the neighborhood, playing in the clubhouse above a garage, in our fortress-style tree house, and at the park. When I learned about the concept of sin in a Sunday-school lecture and searched my memories for when I'd first sinned, I figured it must have been playing doctor in the doghouse with the boys in the community. The lecture told us about Romans 3:23: "We have all sinned and fallen short of the glory of God." After hearing this in class, I prayed to God to forgive my sins. Something about exploring one another's bodies with the plastic stethoscope made me think I'd done something wrong, and prayer didn't help the feeling subside. I felt guilty but wasn't entirely sure why. I used to ask God for forgiveness for my sins frequently. It seemed as if I were part of some sin that was greater than all of us.

Maybe the guilt had to do with my dad's getting in trouble at church. Even he wasn't immune to temptation, it turned out. He was president of Youth for Christ, president of Cair Paravel, and active in the dental association, but he wasn't perfect. He had an affair with his dental assistant, who happened to be married to the pastor's best friend. Plus, the pastor's wife worked as my dad's receptionist. When Mom and Dad went for counseling with the pastor, Dad agreed to repent in front of the church. The pastor told him if he truly asked for forgiveness, the church would forgive him.

One hot, early Sunday morning at my parents' church, I sat with my family in that sanctuary, waiting. Usually kids took church in small classroom settings away from the congregation. That day was different. Strangers came to get Chloe, Erik, and me, to guide us away. I didn't know these adults who led us toward the back of the large linoleum floor, with brown specks and folding chairs laid out in a U shape. But my instincts, even as a six-year-old, told me the look in their eye said they knew something was going to happen and we needed to go. I'd never seen adults act like that—my mother distraught, strangers approaching us kids to guide us away from something. We followed, but not quietly.

"Where're we going?" I asked. "What's happening?"

That morning, my dad repented in front of the entire congregation. The minister called him up to the front of the church. Head hanging low, my dad told the silent audience how he'd strayed in his ways and had an extramarital affair with his dental assistant. He apologized and, with tears in his eyes, asked for forgiveness.

Emotionally devastated, my mother passed out in the sanctuary, collapsing from the intensity of the drama and the summer heat in the poorly air-conditioned building. "Uncle" Carl, Dad's best friend, gathered Mom in his arms and carried her away when the pastor told Dad his plea wasn't good enough. Uncle Carl held my mom as he walked out to the hallway where Chloe, Erik, and I waited. The dense air felt oppressive. He led us to his white Oldsmobile while my father stood before the church. Chloe cried as Uncle Carl carried my mother limp in his arms.

It was quite the scandal for Topeka in the early 1980s when the pastor made an example of my dad, a nice family dentist and professional businessman, and banned him from the church for his affair. They called it an "exfellowship."

My parents' friends gathered close, and most of the people who watched the spectacle quit the unforgiving church and moved on to another Bible church. There were many good folks there, but it was the type of place that performed baptisms in the local lake. The Bible church was part of the revivalist movement—not what I consider a liberal church, but that's the way my parents described it. The church "forgave" my father for his "sins."

When my grandma Ronan, a deeply religious woman, heard this, she scoffed. "I think they're full of themselves," she said, in disbelief that a church would grant forgiveness. In her view, that was God's job, not the minister's.

The split in my parents' relationship and the split in the church also meant splitting the board of the school. The divide in the congregation, and my parents' and their friends' exodus to the Bible church, was a big deal. It meant legal action needed to take place to restructure the Cair Paravel board.

My dad became materialistic and focused on his private dental practice. He compensated for feeling judged by buying things, including a new fur coat for my mom. He bought a new sports car, an RX7. He also bought land in the middle of Kansas. Our family often took road trips out there; I dressed in tight jeans and cowgirl boots, with my favorite black ballet leotard underneath. I still have a Polaroid picture of me wearing that outfit. One time, shortly after the "excommunication," our car got stuck in the mud. We all had to get out of the car. My dad was furious. I remember my mother being afraid. He didn't hit her, but I saw him as a man in the grip of anger. I don't know why he was so angry all the time.

When I misbehaved, I was punished with spanking. It did not deter me. I was a very "strong-willed" child, as some would say. When my parents set rules, I did what they told me not to. I was stuck in middle-child syndrome, and my parents were trying to live up to some really religious standards. They used to read the Reverend Jim Dobson's books about his Focus on the Family and listened when the reverend wrote, "The spanking should be of sufficient magnitude to cause the child to cry genuinely." That didn't work for me; the harder they spanked me, the more entrenched in my emotional stance I became. And beating me with a wooden spoon or a leather belt just strengthened my resolve. I refused to be broken by their tactics when I didn't understand the rules. Finally, my mom learned that if she sat down with me and told me how she felt about what I did and why she didn't want me to do something, I would break down and cry. I wanted to do what was right; I just needed to understand why it was important first.

In 1985, my father split with his business partner, with whom he had practiced dentistry for a few years. My mom became increasingly involved with the everyday management of my father's busy dental office. Business was good. People liked my dad. He was funny and very sociable. I played in the operating rooms and observed many different dental procedures. I rinsed the instruments contaminated with blood in the sink when I was only eight or nine years old. I loved it when the assistants let me help them.

Our family joined the country club, and we started taking swimming and tennis lessons. I was never very competitive. I made my first best friend who wasn't involved with school or church. Her father worked for a local pet-food company, and her bragging rights came from the fact that their house used to be the governor's mansion. It was a fun place to go for sleepovers. We used to stay up watching late-night television on Cinemax, and go swimming in her pool. At night it lit up like a magical aqua bean set in the ground.

At my first slumber party, in the fourth grade, we played the dare game. Somebody dared me to take a midnight swim. That year she and I were tennis doubles partners at the country club. Our motto was that if we couldn't outplay our doubles opponents, at least we could outdress them. Grandma Mera told us, "Girls, you've got to dress to impress."

Grandma Mera played like she was an heiress. She wore cubic zirconias of a size that Flavor Flav, the rapper, would adore. When we went to the country club brunch, she would sing to the music with the pianist hired to serenade our breakfast. Everywhere she went, she acted like she knew everyone. She may have known them, but she also needed to be out with people, even if it was just going to the grocery store. She hated being home.

Just before my grandparents' visit in the fall of 1986, Dad took me and our dog, Sandy, on a walk. "Honey, there are a few things I need to explain about my parents," he said.

"Like what?" I asked.

"Because of living through the Depression and World War II, my parents have different worldviews than your mom and I do, and we agree to disagree on politics and religion," he said.

"What do you mean, Dad?" I asked.

"Well, they are run-of-the-mill Goldwater conservatives. Goldwater ran against Kennedy and didn't win," he said. "My mom believes in God, but not the same way I do. She doesn't believe in thinking negative thoughts; she is a Norman Vincent Peale disciple. As a humanist, she thinks she is a god and told me every day when I was growing up that I was 'God's perfect child.' She kept the good parts of Christian Science and added the ideas of 'positive thinking.'"

"What is Christian Science?" I asked.

"Christian Scientists don't believe in modern medical treatment. Some groups are so extreme that they let people die of preventable diseases." He shook his head. "But it was how she was raised. Great-Grandma Reba was a powerful member of the church in Owosso, Michigan."

"Dad, how come you aren't like Grandma?" I asked.

"Well, in college I joined the campus crusade, and all our friends were part of a Christian Bible study, called Koinonea 'K' Group, at Broadway Baptist Church in Kansas City," he said. "I had an emptiness in my heart that wasn't filled until I started reading the Bible. When my mom and dad get here, let me know if you want to talk about anything they say."

Later that evening, Grandma and Grandpa Mera and their miniature poodle, Sugar, pulled into our driveway in a large recreational vehicle on their way across the country between their "yacht"—which turned out to be a houseboat when we visited them once in Washington State—and their "winter home" in Sun City, Arizona, a small, ranch-style house in a golf retirement community.

In 1987, my parents sold our little house on Pembroke Lane and we moved to Lagito Lane. The house was on four acres in the country, located across from what was a lake by Kansas standards, but a pond if you're from anywhere else. The land we lived on looked like Kansas prairie. My parents let the grass in the back two acres go to seed. We rarely left the boundaries of our property. There was a cow pasture just on the other side of a hedgerow at the back of the lot. We were not allowed to trespass on the neighbor's farm. Instead, we played on the swing set and spent hours videotaping each other and playing around the house. Chloe liked to have me videotape her while she acted out her favorite Michael W. Smith songs. I still tease Chloe about making me film her for hours on end as she lip-synched to Christian rock.

Then there were my mom and dad. The church split. The school board split. The business partnership split. My parents stayed together and had counseling with the pastor every week until the summer before fifth grade, when it came to light that my father was having yet another affair, this time with his new secretary. While staying at my aunt's house in Peoria for a few weeks during school vacation, I got a phone call from my mom. She said there was something she needed to talk to me about. She told me she and my father had separated and were going to get a divorce.

My dad used to have these index cards with pictures of all his goals on them: tropical island vacations, cars, and men and women with perfect bodies. He made goals for each of us in the family scrap-book before he split. He had a blond, perfect model in a bikini in the wife section of his cards. That should have been a clue for all of us that things weren't right. My mom was beautiful, but she would never be short, blond, or petite like the model. The secretary at the dental office, Lydia, looked like my dad's ideal trophy wife.

During our weekly visits with my dad during the separation, we went out to dinner after our tennis lessons at the country club. My dad then drove us around in his oversize Mercedes-Benz. I acted out and told him exactly how I was feeling about this divorce.

"Don't put your hand on the back of my neck," I said, shrugging my shoulders to get my dad's hand off the back of my neck while we were walking to the car after our tennis lesson. "You think you can just pick us up after not seeing us for a week and act like everything is okay?" I said, lashing out at him on the thin sidewalk by the tennis clubhouse.

Dad ignored me, but dropped his hand from my neck, and nodded at another family on their way into the tennis clubhouse.

"It's not okay. You have no right to lie and pretend things are normal. There is nothing normal about seeing you just once a week," I said.

Chloe and Erik felt the same way I did. One time, he put his arm around my car seat. I had wanted to sit in the backseat, but he wanted one of us to sit up front. I was so irritated about his arm being around the seat, I used the electronic seat-position button to get out of his reach. Chloe and Erik watched me, the middle child, reject my dad's affection and started giggling from the backseat. My dad got annoyed at me but also had never had anyone test the limits of the seat posi-tion. He found it as funny as the rest of us by the time I was about a foot off the floor and my face almost touched the windshield.

I wanted him to be part of our family again. Seeing him once a week after tennis lessons was not enough, and pretending like every-one was happy infuriated me. I wanted real love, the unconditional type I heard everyone at church talk about. And I wanted my family back. I shared every dark and angry emotion I had, but I was the only one who did. Chloe and Erik had never tested their relationship with my mom and dad. They always cried when they were punished, and I don't think they wanted to find out whether they would still be loved even if they acted out.

After my mom and dad separated, rumors about my mom and my dad's best friend, Uncle Carl, began. The most hurtful thing happened when Chloe came home in tears after the trip to Lost Valley Ranch with her middle school class. One of her friends told her she wasn't allowed to be around her anymore because of the affair our mom was having with Carl. That was our first clue that maybe he and Mom had something deeper than a friendship. The other kids' parents didn't approve of our family anymore. We were cast out because we were associated with "ungodliness."

That rejection resulted in my wanting to grow up to be different from those people I once looked up to. Being shunned and stigmatized for my parents' behavior isolated me. Now that I was old enough to understand, I knew it was wrong to bear the burden of my parents' actions. People called my mom and told her what she should be doing with her life as a divorcée. Dad sold the house on Lagito Lane, sold the dental practice, and moved away. Then we didn't hear from him for months.

When people asked me how my father was doing, I learned to fight back tears of abandonment. "I don't know," I'd say, and move away from them, blinking back my emotion. At eleven years old, I just wanted to escape that question. Not knowing where he was or what had happened to him split up my heart; I worried about him.

One day, a postcard addressed only to me arrived in the mail. Dad wrote, "Dear Sunny, got hitched to Lydia and found my new life calling as a sea captain. Bought a boat, named it the *Sunny*. Love, Dad."

After that postcard, I had an answer when people asked how my dad was: "He got married and became a sea captain."

Everyone else thought it was funny. They imagined him in floral-print, button-down, short-sleeved shirts and khaki shorts, cruising the Gulf of Mexico with a straw hat to cover his balding hairline and sparse ponytail in the back. He had been telling people for months he wanted to be a sea captain. The dental office staff had even bought him a ship's bell for his goodbye party. But nobody really thought he'd do it. I eventually became flip about it, but at the time, I felt only abandoned and hurt that he had left us to follow a dream. I loved him anyway. I got really good at telling the story, and eventually it didn't feel so traumatic, and I could laugh along with the people I told.

Lydia and Dad had moved to Texas together and bought the boat, the *Sunny*. Lydia fit into his index-card goals, but not enough to last. The yacht was a light-blond powerboat with a small cabin in the bow and a head with a toilet and shower. My dad sent a picture postcard in 1988 from one of the ports near Freeport, west of Galveston, in the Gulf of Mexico, along the intercoastal waterway he called the Ditch. The aerial photograph showed the water stretching across the page horizontally, filling the space. There were little boats floating in the water. I looked to see whether I could find the *Sunny*.

Pregnant

It was just a fantasy, an implausible fantasy. On a Friday night in June 2004, my husband, Jack, and I went out to a little Mexican restaurant in Concord, New Hampshire, for dinner and a few margaritas. By the time we got home, we were up for having sex, but he was so eager to finish that he left me wanting more.

Once he'd fallen asleep next to me, I brought myself to climax on the power of a fantasy. I imagined that a stranger wanted me so badly that he was trying to trick me into getting pregnant and had contaminated my sex toy with his sperm. I'd reached for the pink vibrator and felt it warm and sticky in my mind. The window was open, and an extension ladder stood against the wall leading up to our bedroom. I thought I heard a creak from the ladder outside the window. I had wanted to have a child for a long time, and the idea of this other man—not my husband—being the father turned me on immensely. Maybe I was just drunk, or maybe it was because I was already seeing cracks in my marriage—regardless, I loved the thought, and I recorded the story in my red notebook.

A few weeks later, when I got up one morning, a queasy moment made me think the weather change and pressure were making me dizzy when I got out of bed too fast. It was my day off, and I planned to prepare a special meal for Jack's twenty-seventh birthday. I got up, took a shower, and got dressed, when suddenly flashes of heat came over me in waves, accompanied by nausea. I sat on the floor in the master bathroom and removed my offensively hot and restrictive outfit; I couldn't stand the feeling of the clothes against my skin. As I sat there, pressing my face against the cool tile, I realized I must be pregnant. I did the math and knew my period was late, for the first time in my life, and pinpointed the night of conception to our date at the Mexican restaurant.

By noon the nausea lifted enough for me to put back on my clothes and drive to the nearest grocery store, where I purchased food for dinner and the weekend, and two at-home pregnancy tests.

When I got back home, I peed on the plastic stick with a paper wick at the end. The symbols changed. I could barely concentrate to read the paper instructions, so it took me a while to verify that the symbols meant I was pregnant.

I went to the computer to research the accuracy of at-home pregnancy tests, and when I discovered how high the success rates were, I called the doctor's office and said, "Hi, I'm pregnant; I need to set up a prenatal visit."

"How far along are you?" the receptionist asked.

"I don't know, I just had a positive result with an at-home test kit," I said.

"Let me transfer you to the nurse," the receptionist said.

I waited for a while before they connected me. "May I help you?" a woman asked on the other end of the phone.

"Yes, I'd like to schedule a prenatal visit," I said.

"Before we say you are pregnant, you will need to come into the practice and have a urine test to verify it," the woman said sternly.

"But I already took a test, and it said I was pregnant," I said.

"Well, we have a very accurate test, and need to be certain you are pregnant before we will schedule the prenatal visits," she said condescendingly. The first person I'd told I was pregnant, and already my condition was making me feel invalidated.

We scheduled a test for the next available appointment, and I hung up the phone. For a while, I just sat there and listened to the rain tap against the thick, dense forest leaves out back. The house had no air-conditioning, so the windows were open to the sounds of nature. Thunder crashed in the distance, and my stomach tightened at the thought of Jack flying home in the storm. He was planning to fly into the Manchester airport that evening, following a fishing trip in Canada.

Compounding my anxiety about Jack's flight was my nervousness about motherhood in general. Feeling as if I didn't have permission to share my condition with my network and being alone in rural New Hampshire, with nobody to share my joy and fear with, challenged me in a deep way. I didn't have the skills in place to cope with the isolation. My deepest fear was learning to make it in the world while being responsible for a dependent. As a mom-to-be, I felt overwhelmed by the thought of another person relying on my success to thrive. But my fear soon dissipated as I flipped through the mail that had just been delivered and saw a letter from the University of New Hampshire in the stack. This was what I had been waiting for.

My pulse quickened. I swallowed hard, and everything slowed down as I turned over the letter and opened the sealed flap with my finger. I could feel my pulse keeping slow-motion time in the back of my neck. I tore apart the envelope, pulling the stiff white letter from inside. I scanned the page and found the key word I was looking for: *accepted*.

"We are in, baby!" I said, letting out a squeal of giddy pleasure and excitement. I knew I wanted a change, and between pregnancy and graduate school, I was getting what I wished for. I just needed to convince Jack. I imagined gestating while in classes, studying, and parenting as intellectuals. I wanted to share ideas with my child and feel respected for my knowledge. I saw myself being a mother who was present for her child, just as my mother was always there for me. I wanted so badly to talk to her, but then thought twice and forced myself not to. Jack would be unhappy if he didn't hear first. And when he wasn't happy, he held back emotionally. I couldn't bear the thought.

I'd already tried his cell phone twice, and it was off. It went straight to voice mail. If I kept calling, he'd worry when he powered it on. And then he might be angry with me, and I hated the way his glare felt. Plus, I wasn't going to tell him over the phone. I gritted my teeth and decided to deal with the onset of emotions in isolation, rather than risk the loss of intimacy in our marriage.

I tried to distract myself and do something with the afternoon, but I was glued to my computer that day. I feared the changes that my body would go through. The pain of labor terrified me. I had concerns about the child growing inside me. I worried about the margaritas we'd had the weekend before. I counted every alcoholic beverage I'd had since conception. I mapped it out along the growth and development charts.

That evening, I picked up Jack. "I need to tell you something," I said the second he climbed into the passenger seat after loading up our Ford Explorer, located in temporary parking in front of the terminal.

"What is it?" he asked, closing his door.

"Well, first, I got into graduate school at the University of New Hampshire," I said, pausing to make eye contact. "And I'm pregnant." I started to tear up. "Happy birthday, Jack," I said, and choked on my tears.

"I thought you wanted this," he said, confused by my reaction.

"I do," I said, feeling tears slide down my cheeks. "It doesn't mean I'm not afraid, though."

He reached over and held my hand. I wiped my tears away and drove us home. Mostly we talked finances and income on the drive home; I quoted tuition rates, and we estimated the expenses associated with having a baby and going to school at the same time. When we got home, he held me in his arms and I cried some more. I was pregnant—happy and terrified at the same time.

While we made Jack's birthday dinner, we talked. I convinced him that if we drove our older cars a few more years, we could pay for my graduate school. He called it a "vanity degree," but we made a deal. I would take care of the baby during the day, he'd watch her while I was in school, and we would make it work.

"You can spend an equal amount of our income on guns and things if I can go to graduate school," I said. That sealed the deal for him.

Around the time I started graduate school, I quit my primary job but decided to continue with my volunteer positions and with teaching part-time until the end of the fall semester. Early that fall, I gave my first continuing-education lecture about prenatal health as a mom-to-be. With the organizers watching, I helped keep the presentation going and was asked to speak again at another course. Eventually, I gave the presentation in every corner of the state. I learned all about New Hampshire while driving the tree-lined roads and climbing through the curvy hills and mountains. I loved my time behind the wheel. It was time that was mine. I could think of anything I wanted and enjoy myself. Often I'd envision myself flying next to the car, dancing along the hillsides. It made me feel special.

Early that fall, my stepbrother, Brad, called me several times. He planned to get married. The phone call always had the same ending: "But why won't you come to the wedding? Did I do something to offend you?" he'd ask.

"I'm afraid that something will happen to the baby if I fly," I'd reply.

Whenever I got off the phone with Brad, I found myself having irrational thoughts. One of them was that Brad had placed a curse on me for not going to the wedding. I knew him to be a gentle soul, a warmhearted, kind, and good person. Nonetheless, this idea persisted, as did my inability to articulate what was the matter with me.

During that same time period, guns got between my husband and me, as I began to believe that Jack's hobby was putting the baby and me at risk of lead exposure. All he wanted to do was shoot guns. He tried to convince me that he should build a trench so he could shoot out in the backyard, and he wanted to smelt his own lead bullets after reading about it on an Internet gun forum. But all those ideas concerned me; smelting sounded like a very bad idea, and I knew enough about lead dust to worry when he swept up the brass casings to reload ammunition for his reloading press.

I did my research. I had reasonable arguments. It was a health issue. Jack agreed to go to a physician to get his lead levels checked, but only if he could see a male physician—he said he didn't want another woman to touch him. Meanwhile, I took the basics of my knowledge of infection control and applied them to the lead issue. I asked him to use good decontamination practices, by washing his hands and changing and bagging his clothes before he entered the car after sweeping and getting covered in the lead-filled dust. Then

I'd make him take a shower as soon as he got home. He washed his clothes separately from our other laundry.

He thought I was being neurotic; I thought he was shirking his responsibilities by exposing the baby and me to lead dust. Eventually, he realized I would not budge on this issue, and he also found a lack of support from everyone with whom we discussed the subject, so he agreed to follow my rules, rather than give up his hobby.

We had our first appointment with our new family doctor, Dr. Richard, on a cold day in winter 2005. When we arrived at the medical practice, I wore my heavy black wool coat, sturdy black boots, and maternity pants. I was serious. I wanted to be seen as a family, so I insisted Jack join me for the visit. I also wanted the doctor to talk some sense into Jack about the fact that he was potentially exposing the baby and me to lead from his guns.

We didn't have to wait long in the reception area before a nurse escorted us to an exam room. I took off my coat and climbed up on the exam table; Jack took a seat near the counter.

A nurse poked her head into our exam room. She asked if we'd met the doctor yet. Jack and I both told her no.

"You're going to love him," she said in a conspiratorial whisper.

Another nurse stepped into the room a few minutes later. "Have you met him yet?" she asked. Jack and I both said no again.

"You're going to love him." I was spooked by the way she said it—as if it were a warning.

After that second nurse left, Jack and I turned to each other and chuckled. "I don't know—I'm a little worried about this guy," Jack said.

Neither nurse had heard the other's comment, but we joked about the coincidence. Jack always knew how to make me laugh when I was nervous.

When Dr. Richard walked into the room, the first thing he did was lock eyes with me. I felt as if he knew some secret about me, and it scared me to feel so exposed to a stranger. As soon as that wave of embarrassment hit me, I broke eye contact and quickly turned my eyes to the tile floor in the exam room. *What the hell? Why do I feel embarrassed? What just made me feel so vulnerable?*

"What do you do? Are you working?" he asked me. I tried to be vague.

"I'm in school," I said.

"Oh yeah? What are you studying?" Dr. Richard wanted to know.

I dreaded that question. I wanted to stay anonymous; I wanted to experience the health care system the same way everyone else did. I knew the next words out of my mouth would change the doctor-patient dynamic by exposing my knowledge, and the thought that my providers might grant me special privileges as a result made me very uncomfortable.

"I'm getting my master's of public health at the University of New Hampshire," I said. My whole face was tight with embarrassment. But there it was, like a big elephant sitting in the room.

"Yeah, she just finished a course on environmental health and won't stop nagging me about lead dust and my guns," Jack said.

"Pioneer Sport Club allows only unjacketed lead bullets, and Jack sweeps up the brass casings to reload ammunition. I'm concerned about Jack's exposure to lead and the possibility of passing along that risk to the baby and me," I said, pleading my case to Dr. Richard.

Dr. Richard listened to us argue our stances and agreed there was probably little risk if Jack followed my protocol to reduce our family's exposure.

My new bra seemed to have a mind of its own at that moment. The underwire pressed against my swollen belly, and the ends jutted out in front of my cleavage, creating an unusual effect. The sweater gathered where the underwire poked out and descended into a tented gorge into which the V-neck plunged.

Dr. Richard's gaze fixed curiously on the area. *Maybe he thinks it looks like a third breast*, I speculated. But the more his stare lingered, the more I felt it—and I realized I liked the attention. As his eyes canvassed my body, I felt as if I could hear him thinking, *Your body belongs to me.*

My response to him unsettled me. I wanted a hero to save me from the lead dust, but I didn't want to be attracted to him.

When I tried to explain how I felt to Jack after the appointment, he just got annoyed. "We can go anywhere you want; we've got great insurance," he said.

A few days after the appointment, I stood in my kitchen, contemplating changing to another physician in the group whom we had met earlier in the pregnancy. We had a solid rapport with him, but I was not physically attracted to him. But then I asked myself, *What's the worst that can happen? Why not stay with Dr. Richard?*

"Don't complain, then," Jack said, when I told him I'd decided to stick with our original plan.

What if my feelings were just that? I remembered back to my discomfort with my old boss, back when I worked in Boston in 1999. He unknowingly touched people all over—the lower back, the elbow, the shoulder—guiding them down corridors as if in a dancehall. He'd grown up abroad, and I'd always figured he was just that way. He never meant his touches to come across the way I felt about them—uncomfortable—but he was older than my father, and I didn't like it. It made me think about more than I wanted to with him. At one point, I confided my discomfort to the office manager about all the touching, and he was careful to be more hands-off after that.

But now, in our medical practice, I'd already changed doctors to see the same physician as Jack, and it had created a controversy: letters requesting why we'd made the change, questions from the receptionist. It had felt invasive, and I didn't want it to be a big deal again, so we kept going back to Dr. Richard.

Ever since my belly had started to show in the fall, strangers (all women) seemed to get a kick out of telling me how much pain I'd feel when the baby came. It started to make me fear the birth. I was trying to prepare emotionally for the delivery; I didn't want to be afraid. During one visit, as Dr. Richard and I talked about my birth plan, I explained that I wanted a hospital birth because I was terrified that something could go wrong and I wanted my baby to survive. The thought of a home birth sounded dangerous, and I accepted the idea of preventive surgical intervention if it were indicated. My fear of the pain of labor prompted me not only to sign up for an epidural but also to request a series of topical and cervical injections to numb everything. I didn't want to feel a thing. When I told Dr. Richard how women who didn't know me kept telling me scary stories, he recommended I read Dr. Grantly Dick-Read's book *Childbirth Without Fear*.

When I finally located the dusty old book on the bottom shelf at the library during the start of my third trimester, I thought I must have been mistaken. The leather spine flaked and cracked when I opened it to the first page. I scoffed a little at the suggestion that a text from the 1940s would be relevant today. I thought about putting it back, but instead, I turned the page and started the mysterious recommended reading. By the time I had to leave the library, I'd devoured the classic. Birthing hadn't actually changed all that much—it was just medicine's treatment of it that had changed—and that small treasure of a book changed my orientation to the birthing experience.

I began to imagine it as pleasurable. One passage said the uterus has only one function: to contract. I knew there was another time when the uterus contracted, and that was during the female sexual response cycle. So, to strengthen my uterus for labor, I focused on having better orgasms.

At first it was a secret. I didn't talk about the orgasms, or my strategy, because I was so engorged in the third trimester of my pregnancy that my only relief from the constant blood flow of my swollen clitoris was sexual release in the form of an orgasm. I wasn't working much, I was a graduate student, and I had lots of time on my hands to practice. So I spent my third trimester climaxing in my free time.

The first time I tried out this technique, my body responded quickly. When I climaxed, my baby bump pulled downward as if it were a basketball being dribbled in five steady contractions. It was a shocking physiological phenomenon. Then my baby went still. I worried I'd done something terrible. I lay there and prayed to God that everything would be okay. It took half an hour before I rebounded and felt her move again. When she did, I thanked God and decided I had to try that again.

In 2005, there wasn't much information available about orgasmic birthing, so I didn't really know what I was getting into. By 2013, orgasmic labor was documented in scientific literature in a survey of midwives who had witnessed such births and said they were a matter of anatomy and perception.

As for my anatomy, nobody I know has ever been able to relate to the lurching climaxes I experienced in my third trimester. Labor wasn't pleasurable for anybody else, and even my friends who masturbated said their uterus didn't contract at climax. Nobody in my mother's generation in Kansas talked about sex and masturbation, and she was horrified when I asked if she'd experienced the same phenomenon as I did, so I don't know if the wiring is genetic. But I felt like I was engaging in some sacred secret by practicing my orgasm during pregnancy. There was no contraindication to sexuality that I could find about pregnancy. I'd followed Dr. Richard's orders to read and learn about childbirth without fear; I wanted pregnancy to be fun, to enjoy my body, and to work out my uterus.

At the beginning of March, I sat alone in Dr. Richard's operatory, waiting for him. I'd broken out in an itchy rash earlier that week, and I was miserable. When Dr. Richard examined me, he erroneously and overconfidently misdiagnosed me with pityriasis rosea. I knew it was wrong, but when I gave him a look of doubt, he puffed up and told me a story about another patient of his who'd had the same condition once.

The doctor-patient relationship is a privileged affair. They have total reign over your body. They really can touch every inch of you if they want to. I'd never had a doctor touch me so much; then again, I'd never had to see the doctor every week before. By the time Jack and I went back to see Dr. Richard on Friday, to my embarrassment, Jack noted that PUPPP, also known as the rash of pregnancy, was what I thought it was after my intensive research on Google. "She looked it up and had it right," Jack said. Despite my embarrassment, Dr. Richard corrected his misdiagnosis.

During the whole appointment, Dr. Richard had this sad, heavy look. He'd look me in the eye for a second and then look away, shoulders sagging. I felt sorry for him. I figured he must have to share bad news with someone, but I had no idea that it would be us, until Dr. Richard called later that afternoon and asked for Jack.

Jack's lead levels were high, Dr. Richard told him—anything over ten was high, and Jack was near thirty-five—and those levels were disrupting Jack's kidney function. Even though I now knew my concern was warranted and Jack had indeed experienced high lead exposure from the range, I didn't want to win like that. I wanted the lead to go away and for Jack not to be impacted. I was terrified not only that he'd exposed himself but that he had hurt our daughter and me. I was due in just one week, and I feared that Jack would die and leave me to raise the baby alone.

Fortunately, Dr. Richard played a role in stopping the lead issue from progressing any further. Jack agreed to quit going to the range to stop the exposure from getting worse, and Dr. Richard announced a plan to have both the baby and me screened for lead exposure regularly after the birth.

On my due date, March 11, 2005, I had an office visit with Dr. Richard and experienced a contraction while I was there. When I mentioned it to him, Dr. Richard laid his hands on both sides of my belly and felt the contraction as I sat still on the examination table. His dark blue eyes felt warm and receptive when we connected. He smiled at me with a gentle, kind, knowing look. A wave of something pleasant, almost paranormal, and certainly hormonal, rushed through my veins: sexual attraction to the physician.

Birthgasm

March 2005

The bedroom vibrated. Jack's snowblower pounded against the pavement below our windows. One day past my due date, and we were snowed in. Jack was nervous. He'd told me his greatest fear was to deliver the baby alone with me, using the Internet as a guide. He preferred the idea of going to the hospital.

I woke, reached for my pink plastic–framed glasses, and swept a long strand of hair behind my ear so I could see. Snow clung to the window screens, and I could barely make out the blanketed evergreen forest that encroached on the back of the house. Our wedding photos shuddered in sync with the thunderous noise from his snowblower.

My big belly contracted beneath my maternity sweater when I rolled off the bedding. Dazed by an intense pulling sensation that wrapped itself around me, I held still for a second. The room's walls suddenly felt closer, and my ears pounded. I could have floated if my perceptions had been right. In a gravity-defying motion, I moved my body off the bed. I wanted to know how much snow had come, because I expected my baby girl any day.

Suddenly, warm water gushed down my legs onto my bedroom carpet and my big belly tightened in a steady contraction. I slowed as I crossed the room, and when I turned, I saw a trace of a puddle that turned the mauve carpet dark purple and a trail of wet footprints behind me. I planned to tell the doctor about that contraction. This was different.

Every time I moved, more water flowed down to my soggy socks. I hoped Jack and I would make it to the hospital in time. I tried opening the window to yell out, but the ice had frozen it shut and Jack didn't notice me in the window. Worried the baby would dry out if I kept losing water at the rate at which I was leaking, I continued to the landing of our house and waddled down the stairs. Jack had managed to plow the first pass through the center of the driveway. It would take about an hour before he'd finish his chore, and the snow was still falling. We were snowed in until he was finished. I found the cordless phone on the counter and dialed the doctor's number by heart as I climbed back up the stairs to the master bedroom. There were no signs of blood, so I told myself everything would be okay.

I heard the woman's calm voice from the answering service on the other end of the phone. I took a deep breath before I explained my situation. The woman transferred me to the on-call staff, and I waited for a while before I was connected.

I heard the sound of the snowblower as it kept rattling up and down the driveway. It had grown faint as it went toward the mailbox. At top speed, each pass took about five minutes; then Jack turned about-face and thundered back toward the house, clearing the snow. On the wall, the pictures I'd painted of daffodils in the spring of 2001, the year I won Best Spring Garden in my garden club in Boston, vibrated in response to the snowblower. I took a deep breath and practiced creative visualization as I waited for help. I imagined painting with my little girl someday. The yellow petals contrasted nicely with the energetic blue background, which echoed with traces of light cast diagonally across the canvas. It was one of my best paintings, and I took comfort in the brushstrokes and in thoughts of my future with my daughter.

"Hello?" The sound of a soothing voice answered at the other end of the phone. I knew it was him. I imagined his tall, masculine form seated at a desk, rolling his wedding band in a circle with his thumb and holding the phone to his right ear. A patch of facial hair framed his lips and stretched down his chin, and his rectangular wire-framed glasses and light brown receding hairline made him look like one of the physicians in *Boston* magazine's annual Top Doctors issue.

When I heard Dr. Richard on the telephone line, I leaned back against the headboard.

"This is Sunny Mera. I think my water broke. What do you want me to do?" I asked him nervously.

"How far apart are the contractions?" he asked.

"I don't really know; I haven't timed them," I said. It felt like they were coming frequently, but I'd always been sensitive to changes in my body. I'd felt them come spontaneously for a few weeks. The contractions were gentle and slow and felt comforting to me. They reminded me of the way I felt when I climaxed.

"Why don't you come to the hospital maternity ward, and we'll check on you? Take your time getting here; be careful, and stay safe," Dr. Richard said.

By the time Jack finished clearing the driveway, I'd changed into my favorite herringbone wool maternity pants, with a wide, comfortable, stretchy waistband, and put my suitcase near the door. The minute Jack came inside, I told him I'd already packed our bags and that the doctor had said we needed to go to the hospital. Jack drove me out of the driveway into the middle of a blizzard.

When we arrived at the hospital, we were escorted to an empty maternity ward, where a nurse handed me a hospital gown, then guided Jack and me down the carpeted hallway to the largest, nicest hospital room I'd ever seen and left us alone.

"I think we must have good insurance," Jack said. A rocking chair stood in front of large windows facing east, with a view of a ridge lined with pine trees. There was an armoire with a television, a sleeper sofa, and a convertible hospital bed with a control panel on the side railings.

"I think we got lucky," I said, as I settled in. We talked about our expectations, anticipation, and anxiety surrounding this rite of passage into parenthood, the impending birth of our daughter. We hadn't called anyone to notify them we were going to the hospital. I didn't answer the phone when it rang. This was my secret. It felt safer to guard myself in the private and personal moment of getting ready to give birth. I was one day past my due date, and I didn't want anyone to worry. I couldn't deal with their emotions when I was dealing with my own.

The storm got worse. At least eight inches of fresh snow had fallen overnight. Another two inches of thick snowflakes clustered on the sill just outside my window while we waited.

My labor progressed slowly. Dr. Richard reassured me and encouraged a little exercise to speed things up. When we walked around the maternity ward, I found myself listening for Dr. Richard's hypnotic voice in the echoes of the hospital's hallway. I searched for his presence, and that scared me even as I fantasized about the way his touch felt.

Jack didn't touch me enough, and our sex life had changed. He liked it rough, so when the sex got uncomfortable during my pregnancy, most of the time I gave to Jack orally, and the intimacy that had bound us turned into distance. I worried that he would be unfaithful, but maybe it was my own lack of connection I should have worried about. There was not enough of one to bind me to Jack in the face of my forceful attraction to Dr. Richard.

My baby girl kicked throughout the whole labor. I thought she was awake because she was used to contractions and orgasms. As the contractions intensified, I asked for a yoga mat. The nurse brought me a thick gym pad instead. I sat with my legs in the lotus position and ran my thumbs along the soles of my feet to soothe myself. When Dr. Richard came in to check on us for the last time that night, he wouldn't stop watching my hands stroking my feet. I felt self-conscious about the way he looked at me. I still was not in active labor, but I had started to sense the power of the contractions. The stronger they got, the more they reminded me of what I had read about pregnancy orgasms. I started to feel sexually aroused. It felt faint and distant, but I became less comfortable with having Dr. Richard in the room.

His voice cornered me. It was the only thing I could hear. Dr. Richard talked about his favorite pastime with the staff at the nursing station.

"I play word games. My favorite uses palindromes. I like to say things that have special meaning backward," he said.

When I heard Dr. Richard's voice and his story about playing with words, a primitive part of me awakened to the idea of his favorite game, with the palindromes, and put me under his control in that vulnerable moment. In my sacred space, I became transfixed by the game and by Dr. Richard. He had me. I was *his* patient, like some tribal lord's property in the kingdom of Hospital Land. And I felt an animalistic allegiance to his aura. Those words about his favorite game haunted me.

The nurse applied pressure to my lower back to ease the intensity of the contractions while I vomited in a basin from the intense rush of hormones and changes my body was going through. When I felt Jack come to my side, he extended his arm to be there for me, but his touch felt like torture on my burning skin and I rejected him with a sharp "don't." As I pushed Jack's hand away from me, I saw Dr. Richard watching us from across the room. Our eyes met, and he didn't look away. He should have, but he dominated me with those eyes of his. He made me feel things I wasn't prepared to feel.

As my labor progressed, the contractions felt more and more like orgasms. Jack stayed in the room with the nurse and me the whole rest of the day and night. He slept on the sofa until I went into active labor. For two or three hours after the transition, I breathed deeply, like I'd learned in yoga training in my early twenties. I rode waves of pleasure in counterpoint to the intense contractions. Birthgasms. It was like tripping on drugs—experiencing the most intense and hallucinogenic ecstasy of my life—only it was natural.

I moved about the room until I discovered sitting was the most comfortable position for me. At dawn they brought me a birthing chair, and I changed into a light blue hospital robe. I faced the panoramic view of rolling hills still cloaked in darkness. Jack wanted to watch the sun rise and had left the blinds open, until the nurse convinced him that in my state I'd do better with darkness. Jack stayed by my side as the nurse applied pressure to all the right spots on my back and brought a damp cloth to help me regulate my temperature.

I struggled to make sense of my experience and didn't have words to articulate my feelings. I wanted Dr. Richard, even if it was inappropriate. I felt guilty and confused by my response to the erotic experience of the labor.

I heard the door open as Dr. Richard returned to my room in the morning. Going with the flow, letting the feelings wash over me in waves, I sat on the birthing chair. With my eyes closed, I breathed slowly and deeply, feeling the ebb and flow of painful contractions and euphoria. I saw a pulsing lotus flower floating in my third eye. Vibrant and ephemeral, the blossom emanated sparks of light and energy. Black flirted at the edges of my vision, creating a border, a periphery of darkness.

I went inside myself. My eyes were closed. I didn't want to look the physician in the eye again. But I could hear his black leather shoes click against the linoleum tile floors on his way to where I sat.

I knew it was wrong that I liked to fantasize about Dr. Richard sometimes—I wanted to be feeling those urges toward my husband, who was sitting right next to me—but I couldn't go back and take those fantasies away. Dr. Richard was so good-looking, and he was so nice to me. My eyes closed and focused on my third eye; the power inside felt primitive, like an animal's instinctual urges. The vision of the pulsing lotus flower shooting sparks of light stopped when I opened my eyes.

I felt present in the moment the way you feel when you wake from a deep sleep or heavy meditation. My eyes opened and focused on Dr. Richard, and I willed him to leave to protect myself from desire. It was my last line of defense. When I looked into his eyes, he was so empathetic, it flooded my senses. I was afraid to feel my attraction for him in the most vulnerable moment of my life. I'd never felt anything like it before, and I didn't know how to block him out. My eyes were my only means of telling him to go.

He jumped back a bit when our eyes met this time but said, "It's time to check on your progress. You'll have to lift the gown and spread your legs apart so I can examine you."

I complied. Lifting the gown up, tucking it between my breasts and belly, I spread my legs wide on the seat. Dr. Richard put on blue nitrile gloves and turned to the overseeing physician.

"I just go back and forth to get in, right?" Dr. Richard asked another provider observing him. I heard his words again in my head. *Go back and forth. Back and forth to get in.* I smirked. I amused myself with the fantasy Dr. Richard would pass over my clitoris using this back-and-forth technique. After all, my clit was so engorged, how could he not touch it?

Once the gloves were on, he got down on one knee before me. I took a deep breath. Dr. Richard stabilized himself by putting his left hand on my right knee. His right hand went between my thighs. It was a moment in time where my idle imagination met a stiff clinical reality. With my husband at my side, one part of me was next to him and another part of me was in another world, some magical land with intensely rich internal sexual stimuli. Dr. Richard's right hand was my portal between the two realities. I didn't know where the fuck I was when he touched my core.

It was the best and worst thing that had ever happened to me. I felt his fingers sweep back and forth against my clit. He slowly entered me, using this technique over and over again. He reached my G-spot, and I felt his forceful twist as his hand slid deep inside me. All the while, I felt the pressure of his grasp on my other knee. I could feel him watching my every breath. I tried to deny my soft moan as he touched me deeply.

He explored my cervix carefully, then took his other hand to press down on my belly. It stung. As his index finger swept the membrane around the cervix, I winced.

He removed his hands from me. "You're not ready," he said. I lost my composure and started to faint. As I began to collapse toward Jack, he reached out his arms to steady me.

The nurse rushed to my side. "It's okay, you'll be delivering before you know it," she said encouragingly. Dr. Richard had stepped away to remove his gloves but turned, surprised at the commotion, and cocked his head to the side at the sight of my swoon.

I felt devastated in response to his exam and discouraging words. Thoughts rushed through my mind in a stream of consciousness that I could not control. The labor, in particular the touch of the physician, was a seminal event that started my cascade into a dysfunctional brain disorder or illness that included romantic, erotic delusions of a relationship with Dr. Richard.

Why did he touch me like that? Why did he go back and forth so

*many times over my clit? Did a man I'm physically attracted to just
finger me like that in front of an audience? Nobody has ever touched
me like that before, and everyone acted like nothing happened? How
did he know my G-spot? Did he intentionally touch me like that?*

*I want him. What if he wants me, too? But it's clinical; he can't want
me—he's Dr. Richard. I can't feel like this. I need to want Jack. Jack is
the one whom I should be feeling this for.*

I tried to deny my urges; it was an impossible fantasy to be wanted
by Dr. Richard. Yet I felt euphoria like I'd never known at the thought
of him. I wanted to belong to him.

After the exam, I sat and progressed through labor with my eyes
closed, feeling the intense contractions pass over my body in waves.
For an hour I sat and breathed through these orgasmic contractions.
The sparks of light in the center of the lotus flower intensified. I had
never done hallucinogenic drugs, but I'd read descriptions of opium
dens inhabited by lotus eaters. When my pain pathway took me there,
I figured I knew the same paradise addicts experienced. I sat and felt
my body swallow up my thoughts like the tide rushing over a bed
of sea creatures, pulling them from the shore. My mind lifted and
flowered in another world, a land between reality and fantasy, my
internal paradise. It was the place where the lotus flower streamed
pulses of light. It was beautiful, but after he touched me, I was different. I couldn't let the memory of his touch go. His presence haunted
me. It was too much. In my sacred space, I felt him near me and I
wanted him. Anyone else's presence wouldn't have gotten into my
sacred space that way, but his touch had left me burning with desire.

My hips began to feel heavy as I sat on the chair. By the end of
the hour, I could feel my baby girl move down my body. I was almost
ready to deliver, so I moved from the chair to the bed. I wanted to
deliver with dignity, and somehow the thought of Dr. Richard crawl-
ing on the floor wasn't dignified. I tried to pretend he wasn't present,
but he was all I wanted to sense in the room.

Jack trailed behind as I moved across the room. Once I was up on
the bed, he reached out over the bedrail to hold my hand. I started to
kiss his hand in a passionate way. It all felt so intense to me; I wished
we could be together the way we'd made the baby, but all eyes were on

us. I rolled toward Jack and buried my face in his hands, kissing his palms madly. I wanted to erase everything Dr. Richard made me feel: pleasure, disappointment, and now embarrassment.

I pulled Jack's hand to my mouth. I felt the urge to bear down on something, and Jack's hand was right there.

"She bit me!" Jack exclaimed, looking over me to Dr. Richard.

"Oh, I didn't mean to," I said in a desperate voice. I felt out of control. "I'm so sorry." I had tried to hold back the urge to bite hard, but my actions were primitive.

As the baby descended in my body, I felt the tears roll down my cheeks, and I winced in pain. "Slow and easy," Dr. Richard coached, but it was too late—I wanted to be done. It was my time to deliver, and my internal sensations were impossible to deny. I listened to my needs. I felt an internal craving to bear down. I pushed hard. Seconds later, Dr. Richard caught my baby's perfect little body in his arms.

How It Came to Be

Minutes after the birth, the blinds went up. The staff let Jack open them to the winter scene outside. It was eleven o'clock on Sunday morning. I listened as Celtic music played on the same radio station I'd tuned the night before to pop music. The nurses had asked Jack a few times if I was Irish. He'd said no but had missed the hint that the music might be untraditional during a hospital birth. The chanting of new-age Celtic music in the dim, cloaked room where I would go back to visit in my memories for years to come was inaudible to Jack. Songs like "The Mystic's Dream," by Loreena McKennitt, played as I lay, still deeply inside myself but being brought out into the break of light.

As I opened my eyes, I felt as if something was missing. I froze with panic. Where was my baby? She was no longer part of me, but I oriented toward her cries. The nurse stood at the counter, measuring. I looked across to my baby, trying to feel a connection. I'd read that I would feel an instant attachment. I searched inside for that feeling, but instead I felt an absence of the intrinsic bond we'd shared earlier.

When they laid my baby on my chest, the nurse asked what the baby would be named. "I like the name Jamie; I think she looks like a Jamie. And someday I want to give her a brother named Sam," I said, looking through my lashes at her lying on my chest. We'd already picked names.

"How did I do?" I asked Jack. I struggled to remember what had happened during labor, because no one else seemed to be disturbed by my recollection of how Dr. Richard had examined me.

"You did great." He sighed and smiled. "You make me so proud," he said. He looked into my eyes. "That other lady down the hall was screaming so loud, it sounded like a horror show," he teased, then proudly snapped a photo of his two girls. It was the only picture he ever took of me with Jamie. I was too tired to look up, but he caught my smile and Jamie's squishy face, so perfectly alarmed to be out of the womb. Her small cries sounded painful and filled me with a deep sense of anxiety, until she fell asleep on my chest. We were both drowsy. I lay flat on my back with Jamie snuggled up between my breasts, with warm blankets layered over us.

Dr. Richard came over to say goodbye.

"That was amazing. Once it's over, everything is fine," I said.

His eyes glistened as he drifted back toward me.

"Yes, and everything *is* fine. I promise I'll check on you tomorrow," he replied gently.

Just looking into his eyes soothed me. I nodded in response, unable to articulate anything else from the complicated mess of emotions starting to bubble up. Knowing he would come to me helped me feel secure, but I felt the loss of my pregnancy. I missed having Jamie as a part of my body. Nobody had told me that could happen. I wasn't close enough or connected enough with her. It was not enough for me. Jamie couldn't communicate except to cry. The distance between us when I was holding her in my arms devastated me. When I held my baby, she did little more than sleep, cry, and nurse. I expected a baby like you see in the movies: alert, happy, and interactive.

After the labor, the nurse brought two large ibuprofen tablets with a cup of water. "Here, you should take this," she said. It was the first medication I'd taken since I'd arrived at the hospital after my water broke.

I slept with Jamie on my chest. I kept hearing staff members' whispers.

"It was natural," one nurse told the other at the change in shifts. I breastfed Jamie as the nurses instructed me to do. But I struggled to wake every time she needed me. The loss of sleep from the labor had worn down my stamina.

In the middle of my first night of motherhood, a nurse came in to wake me. "Your daughter needs you," she said.

"Why?" I asked in a foggy haze.

"She needs you to nurse her, and you need to wake up when she's crying. This is your job, not mine." The night-shift nurse shamed me for not being able to wake up and respond to my daughter, when my milk hadn't even come in yet. I wanted to tell that nurse she was wrong. I wanted to say, *I need sleep, and it is in fact your job to give me a break while I recover from the birth.* But I didn't say anything, and I felt like a failure as a mother.

The next day, Dr. Richard never came. By 5:00 p.m., another resident came to check on me. When I looked into her eyes, I knew. She loved Dr. Richard, too. Our eyes connected like we were both in a trance. I fought to gain control over my feelings of abandonment when she told me he couldn't come to see me but that she was there instead. I don't remember if she examined me or even touched me, but I looked into her soul and knew I wasn't the only one who felt like this about him.

Those first two days in the hospital, we never let Jamie leave the room. I had read stories about hospital mix-ups, and I would not risk my baby's being lost and getting stuck with someone else's mother. When we did take Jamie for her hearing test, both Jack and I escorted her crib down the hall.

By the third day, I started to get into a routine. I showered and learned the basic skills of swaddling, and began breastfeeding, diaper changing, and holding, rocking, and just staring at my baby. I held Jamie in my arms as she latched on and suckled at my breast. I watched her connect with me and began to feel that stir of motherly emotion, but I still couldn't totally distract myself from the memory of what had happened with the touch of the physician and how I felt about it.

I tried to connect with people when they came to visit, but I struggled to stay in the moment. I was too caught up in trying to come to terms with having experienced the most intense sexual encounter of my life. To make matters worse, it had been clinical; I hadn't had permission to enjoy it the way I had my earliest sex with Jack.

I met Jack in the spring of 1994, during a high school musical production of *Fiddler on the Roof.* I was the spotlight operator, and he was the lighting director. I watched him as he gave instructions to someone managing the stage crew while he wound up a bright orange extension cord, and he was so bold and confident that I thought, *I could listen to him for the rest of my life.*

We had our first conversation over headsets. He tried to explain how to change the gels in the spotlight. I had never used a spotlight before, so this was a new learning experience, but after his explanation I felt moderately informed about how to run a spotlight. I did ask for help from him to change the gels for the first time, and that is how we met face-to-face.

A few months later, Jack stopped me on the stairs between classes and asked if I'd like to go out with him. For our first date, I met him at my favorite hangout, a coffee shop downtown. The inside of the coffee shop had exposed, raw wooden beams, plastic chairs, and tables with vinyl tablecloths. I knew all the regulars there and often sat and talked with them at one of the back tables to pass time. Jack, however, was not impressed by the location, and made multiple disparaging remarks about the decor and the patrons. I couldn't help but feel offended. Looking back on his behavior, I think he was trying to impress me by how cool he was. When we parted that evening, I felt put off, but I hadn't completely abandoned my hopeful vision of an infinite future.

So when Jack called to invite me to a concert, I agreed. He got the tickets as a birthday present. We held hands walking into the concert. When we saw people we recognized, I dropped his hand. The public display of affection made me feel like a "sinner," and I blushed with shame. Because I grew up going to Bible school, my emotions about sin and sexuality were complicated. I'd come of age with the stigma of the scandal that split the school my parents started in my family's attic. I wanted to rebel against the people who stigmatized us and made us feel unloved, but the views the Bible school had taught me still influenced me.

After the concert, Jack drove me in his red Mustang to a drive-in burger joint. As we sat in the car, waiting for our burgers and ocean-blue sodas, Jack reached for my hand. "You were ashamed to hold my hand earlier," he said.

"It wasn't that. Those kids went to Bible school with me when I was younger. All the crap that they filled our minds with about sin came flooding back." I reached over and stroked his hair.

"I don't believe you," he said, continuing to hold my other hand.

"Jack, it's different when we aren't in public—I can be myself with you. But when we're in a group . . . I was just socialized differently. I mean, have you ever been to the Bible church?" I asked.

"Yes, and I will never go back," he replied. He described having witnessed a baptism in a lake. A girl he'd met had taken him there to try to "save" him, but he'd been too dense to realize her motive until he got there.

I laughed at his funny story, and when our burgers arrived, he told me he almost went to Cair Paravel, a private Christian school where the Bible church people went. But his dad, a Brooklyn Jew, didn't feel comfortable with it, so he never went.

"You know that school started in my family's attic, right?" I asked.

"Really?"

"Yeah, it's funny how everyone likes to say how it was named after the castle in C. S. Lewis's *Chronicles of Narnia*, but they skip over the history of Cair Paravel and my parents' cultish bible study, the K Group, named for Koinonea, a fellowship. They'd love to forget the part with the scandal that split the school board." Between bites I added, "Did you know a church exfellowshipped my father for having an affair? It was sorta like an excommunication. He was banned from the church. All my parents' friends, the group who founded the school, gathered near and changed churches to the Bible church, which forgave my father for his sin. It took legal action to split the board, but the school lived on. It's still graduating kids, training classical Christians. It's a mind-fuck of an education, if you ask me."

"How so?" Jack asked.

"Well, they teach you to have blind faith yet question everything," I said.

"Hmm, close your eyes," he said. I shut my eyes, and Jack kissed me.

"What was that for?" I asked.

He just smiled.

That summer of feeling loved by Jack was the best I'd ever felt. Our "first time" happened in his basement bedroom. I'd been reading novels about this moment for years, and I was filled with anticipation. I desperately wanted to lose my virginity, and I didn't feel like a sinner when I was in Jack's bedroom with him.

We debated our music selection prior to intercourse. I wanted to listen to something memorable, like the *Twin Peaks* soundtrack, but when we went to play it, Jack laughed and said no. Instead, he played Jackopierce's song "Along for the Ride." We'd broken his bed while playing around earlier in the week, so I sat on the mattress on the floor where the bed used to be.

Jack came to me and started to kiss me. I participated curiously, letting him take the lead. The lights were off, so I studied the flashing lights on his computer and his amperage rack filled with equipment. I felt my need build.

"Please . . . take me," I begged.

He thrust into me hard, and I gasped at the intensity of him, but it wasn't painful, since I'd started preparing the year before by masturbating. For the first time, I felt completed being with him like that. I wanted him. I loved the feeling of the intimacy of sex. When Jack climaxed seven minutes later, I felt a gentle wave of something pass over me as I stared at the digital clock above the blinking equipment lights. I wasn't sure what to call the warm feeling that spread over my body. It wasn't hard and fast, but it was pleasurable.

He rolled off and put his arm around me. I asked for him to hold me for a while, and he did. After the album ended, we got restless. Mostly we didn't say much after we did it. It wasn't as glamorous as I'd expected it to be, but it felt right having sex; he was nice to me, and that was what I liked. Even if we didn't agree on anything, our physical connection was intense.

Giving birth was a sexual experience for me. When I say this, people reel back; they don't want to hear it. But how could pushing something that big out of my vagina not have been sexual? My dilemma was that nobody else gave me permission to experience my journey the way it happened for me. I was touched by the one person in the hospital I felt attracted to, who should not have touched me, and then I was hushed up, cast out, because of my minority opinion on birthing. It took years to find my voice, but my story was impossible to suppress. It needed a way out of me.

At first, I was not at peace with my experience, and I didn't know how to bring it up naturally, so I tried simply to accept the burden. But not having a method to relate my story isolated me. I wanted to feel loved and to enjoy myself. I wanted Dr. Richard to accept me, but instead I felt like I threatened his career. Overall, I didn't blame him; it wasn't his fault that our system is broken, and that I found him attractive as a person. We were just two people, and everybody has flaws. Why did someone, somewhere, decide it was right to accept a pretense that doctors aren't people and patients aren't people and there is some construct that separates us?

I tried to ignore my feelings and put aside Dr. Richard's back-and-forth technique. It was part of a standard of care to perform an exam, and I sat in such a way that he couldn't access my vagina easily. It was the only place I was comfortable. I just wished he had asked me for permission to give me that exam. Instead, he simply told me it was time. If he had asked for my permission before he touched me, would I have been able to shake my head back and forth or say no? Would that have been allowed? I had tried to tell him with my eyes. I wanted to be a good wife and instinctually knew my attraction to the physician trumped my feelings for my husband.

I struggled in my isolation to process my intense experience. I was afraid to get the physician in trouble. I loved him as a person. I didn't want to hurt him. Because of my desire for him, I felt guilty. In my emotional mess of feelings, I had a sense of loyalty to him. But I so needed to feel comforted. I wanted Dr. Richard to want me, or at least to understand the ramifications of his examination for me as a person, not just as his patient.

I've read physicians are trained to treat patients as something other than the people they are, and doctors are supposed to act like they aren't flawed humans. Sometimes I wonder, if that construct had been removed and he had asked my permission to touch me, like every other man in my sex life had, whether things would have been different for me. All my power to protect my sacred space was taken from me by our medical system when I was assigned to the role of patient.

My mom came out from Kansas to help after Jamie was born. I needed help. It was my first experience taking care of a newborn. None of my brothers, sisters, cousins, and few friends had children yet, and I didn't even know how to change a diaper. I relied on my family for support. I didn't share my mother's faith or have support from a spiritual community, yet I longed to feel as if I belonged.

That desire only intensified in 2005 after Jamie's birth. I relied on my mom to teach me how to give the baby a bath, hand-express milk from my breasts when they became engorged after my milk came in, and learn to listen for what different cries sounded like. What did a hungry cry sound like? What did a tired cry sound like? I tried to listen, but for me a crying baby's cries just sounded like a crying baby.

Those first days, hours, and weeks, I wore Jamie in a sling next to my chest. Body against body. It bonded us. Jamie was happy whenever she was held close.

My mom stayed for over a week. Jack was ready for her to depart by the end of it. He had two weeks off from work but hid in the basement.

"Is everything okay with Jack?" she asked.

"Yeah, he just gets like this when people are around for a while. Remember Thanksgiving?" I asked.

"Yes, I know, you told me. He was hiding," she replied.

"Well, I think having company around is getting to him, and that's why he stays in the basement while you're here. I mean, not that he spends that much time with me when you aren't here, but it's not as noticeable. He at least will finish his dinner before heading downstairs when he is with me. And with Jamie, I think we need some space to adjust," I said.

"Oh, honey, I don't mean to make things hard on you by staying. It's just that I want to be here for you and your baby," my mom said.

"I know, but I think it's time for you to go, Mom. It will be okay," I said.

So Jack went back to work and my mom returned to Kansas. That left me alone with Jamie in that big house.

Slowly, my perceptions were changing. Nobody was aware of the significance of those changes. After my mom left, I soon found that the simple act of walking around the house, holding Jamie, was the easiest method to soothe my baby. Jamie didn't like to be set down. She wanted to be with her mommy at all times. So I would walk laps around the first floor.

Our house stood on two acres in a small town. It was a large lot joined at the back to a spread of open land, in a friendly neighborhood. We had made acquaintances with the neighbors, but the homes were so spread out, I didn't bump into people, except a few times running errands or when I took walks with Jamie around the block, up to where I could look out over the rolling hills toward Concord.

When I saw my neighbors, it was a relief to have someone to spend a few minutes with, catching up, hearing about the movements of local wild turkeys, fisher cats, and flying squirrels. But it wasn't like I saw a neighbor every day. Walking daily without seeing anyone reminded me of how isolated our home was. If I did go out to the grocery store, it was a twenty-minute drive. When I got there, people were friendly enough, but in a way that made me feel lonelier. It reminded me I didn't belong to the community. Being alone with my baby made me feel vulnerable and trapped in my thoughts, and that took its toll over time.

Constant Little Reminders

Something happened with our phone service in the spring of 2005, about a month before Jamie was born. The phone rang often.

"Is Sharon there?" a strange man's voice would ask.

"You must have the wrong number," I'd say. Then I'd hear the line click silent.

As time went on, I wondered who Sharon was. I was busy studying, so I didn't spend too much time preoccupied by the wrong-number calls. Somebody somewhere must have given out the wrong number.

But after Dr. Richard's story about palindromes during my hospital stay when I gave birth, I began to wonder if he was sending me secret messages. When I got the call for Sharon, I interpreted it as an anagram, "no rash." That was the name the calls asked for before I developed the rash of pregnancy. Or was he sharin' with me? Get it—"Sharon"?

Once Jamie was born, the wrong-number calls slowed down. But one day while my mom was still visiting, the phone rang.

"I'll get it," my mom said. "Hello?"

"I'm sorry, there is no one here by that name," she said. She hung up the phone. "Huh, wrong number." She shrugged her shoulders and came back to sit near me on the rocking chair as I sat in my favorite spot on the sofa, near the window. I tensed up when I heard her say "wrong number."

"Who did they ask for, Mom?" I tried to ask casually.

"They wanted to speak to Karen," she replied.

"Karen." I thought immediately that he was carin' for me, as I repeated "Karen" softly. But it was too far deep to tell my mom that I thought Dr. Richard was sending secret messages.

As Jamie's first summer progressed and the problems with the feeding intensified. Jamie would pull away from my breast and cry after just a few seconds of eating. As my stress about Jamie not gaining weight increased, so did the wrong-number calls for Karen. By the end of the summer the name changed again, this time they asked for "Korin".

When I heard the strange voices on the other end of the phone asking for Korin, I worried Dr. Richard might be obsessive-compulsive, particularly with his anagrams. Was I "near OK"? Or, I wondered, was I part of some "core" and I was "in"? I looked up a few of the phone numbers that were listed on the phone bill; they came from Republican Party members and the phone company. I searched the Internet and felt more paranoid. If I hadn't believed in those calls' meaning something, I would not have attached such significance to other events, but the phone calls made me buy into the idea that Dr. Richard loved me and was using his connections in politics to connect to me, or that there was a conspiracy unraveling around me. He was politically active, but so was everyone in New Hampshire. Dr. Richard's love for humanity appealed to me intensely. I struggled to let go of the bond. Especially when I thought the random-number calls were from Republicans carin' for me, or, even creepier, that they were "near K."

But every thought led back to Dr. Richard. I wanted so badly to get away from the memory of him that I planned as many activities as possible to keep my mind occupied. I met some moms at a baby yoga class, and they invited me to another playgroup. There, I got to know other women with babies the same age.

I couldn't help but talk with my friends about what was going on and why I felt like a daily failure as a mother and wife. It was the little things: forgetting the blanket to lay down for the baby to crawl on, when all the other moms protected their babies from the grass and pine needles; not knowing how to handle the awkwardness of having a fussy baby in public when nothing seems to soothe your child.

I shared with anyone I thought would be willing to listen: the playgroup, some of the moms' club members, some of the people I met on the playground, some of my friends from classes at school, my old friends from high school, and family. What I learned, from how these people responded to my birthgasm story, was that every new mother could relate to the trauma of childbirth, and many supported me in my journey to make sense of what happened. Many of the mothers had their own issues. Whether it was getting slammed with Pitocin, not having the pregnancy they envisioned, having an unplanned cesarean, not getting the epidural they wanted, or having some other intervention unexpectedly given or withheld, we were all left "touched" by childbirth. Our expectations and the reality of the experience were rarely well matched.

Going to graduate school helped me stay sane. It was my only adult interaction on days there were no playdates, doctor's visits, or moms' group meetings. I never missed a class in my public health program. Waiting for Jack to get home, when I didn't have a packed schedule, made me feel desperate. I'd sit in the living room, looking out the bay window, waiting for him to turn up the long, stone wall–lined driveway. I cooked things he liked from *Bon Appétit*. On nights I didn't have class, I'd cook filet mignon with a mustard sauce, served over spinach; rack of lamb with rosemary and garlic, served with roasted vegetables; beautiful salads tossed with specialty cheeses and homemade dressing; and fresh-baked breads from the store. I tried to be a good housewife, but I never felt like one. Jack wasn't happy; he came home irritated.

"I really just want some alone time," he would say, when he walked in the door and found me waiting for him. He was with people all day, so he really wanted some space, while I needed interaction.

"Come upstairs," I pleaded at the top of the stairs one night, needing to connect to try to escape my thoughts about the birthgasm. The sound of his computer game as he attacked the enemy rumbled in the air.

"What?" He removed the headphones that played music beneath the loud rumble of the game.

"I want company. Come hang out with me," I said, as I bowed my head down the stairs to see him. The basement was dank, with concrete floors and an exposed ceiling of insulated rafters held up by metal piers.

Jack finished and saved the game before untwining the wires, attached to large, padded earmuffs, from around his neck. He followed me into the kitchen, where I had lit a candle and set out two wineglasses. I handed him the bottle of red and the heavy wine opener.

I watched him pull out the cork and start to pour. "Ever since the birth, I can't stop thinking about it," I began.

"Yeah, I got it. You've already told me about it," he said.

"I just want help to work through it." I looked into his dark brown eyes behind his black metal–framed glasses.

"Can't you just forget about it?" he asked, as his eyes grew cold and he glared at me.

A wave of emotion in response to his rejection of my experience passed over me, and I said, "No, I can't stop thinking about it." I felt tears begin to well up, and a salty taste in the back of my nose. "I need your help. I want you to work through it with me. I think if I could just reclaim the experience, it would help." I tried not to sound as desperate as I felt.

"What do you mean?" he asked seriously.

"I want your help to go back into the memory and reclaim it. Sorta like role-playing. You could be the physician, and we could go through it together," I said, envisioning someone loving me through the experience, wanting me in that moment in time. I needed to reclaim my mind from the memory of Dr. Richard's touch, to take back my experience from his presence, and I wanted to do it with someone I loved.

"I'm not going to pretend I'm Dr. Richard. This isn't what I agreed to when we got married," he chided me snidely. "It's too kinky." He took a sip of wine, then glared at me again and said, "Why can't you just be normal?" I felt his anger and annoyance seething from his every movement. His body was tense and unforgiving. He had no empathy, and I knew from his expression that my obsession with the physician wounded him deeply.

"You don't understand—I need you to help," I pleaded, wanting so much to find something better than a birth experience where I was touched clinically to be my most profound sexual experience. I fought back tears. "Please help me, love me through this," I begged.

"No," he said, and, holding his glass of wine, turned back toward the basement.

Eventually he forbade me to talk about my orgasmic labor or even to mention Dr. Richard. Our sex life returned to normal within two months. "Normal" was vaginal intercourse with little foreplay and no aftercare. It worked for him. Jack's anger at my desire for the physician ate at my heart as he pounded his hardness into me. Jack's wanting me helped a little, but his anger left me feeling empty. After Dr. Richard's touch, because it was clinical and unintended, I felt deeply unwanted.

Still, Dr. Richard's influence dominated everything I touched, everything I thought, everything I did. I didn't care if it was an accident. I wanted the lusty memory, because it was so powerful for me. It created very real, very strong emotions. I liked it. It aroused me. In rural New Hampshire, he was my primary care provider; he provided all our family's health care services. So I saw him for everything. As my postpartum exam day neared, I created an entire fantasy about it. I wanted Dr. Richard. I imagined being in the stirrups with his head between my thighs as he studied me. Then, slowly, Dr. Richard touched me and pulled back my labia. I felt aroused and watched him insert his hard metal device, sitting up on my elbows. Watching him watching me. It did it for me every time.

When I arrived for the postpartum visit, our eyes locked and I must have looked desperate for him. His gaze slid to the wall, and he suppressed a smile. His exam was totally professional and quick, but Dr. Richard said something about my labor.

"The nurse knew how to touch you right," Dr. Richard said, referring to the woman who helped me through the labor.

The unspoken look in Dr. Richard's eye suggested he knew that Jack didn't know how to touch me. He exposed my sexually unsatisfying relationship with Jack, and it scared me that anyone knew that Jack didn't touch me right. When Dr. Richard referred to how

I liked to be touched, it frightened me, because I couldn't forget the way he had touched me. His six to ten strokes, with that back-and-forth technique, had been so powerful that I couldn't forget them. I still felt him touching me at times. The experience was burned into my memory. The pleasure of his touch washed over me in waves, and his reference to how I liked it nailed me.

After a physical exam, physicians always want to ask about sex. That was the first time I relaxed during the whole appointment. We were standing at the exam table while he held Jamie's feet. He was stroking the soles of my baby's feet. It was beautiful to watch how happy it made her. Her reflex to spread her toes was perfect.

"Try to go easy at first. There are alternative ways to find pleasure," Dr. Richard said about resuming marital relations. He smiled to himself after he said it. I was speechless. How dare he prescribe how my husband and I behave in the bedroom? Plus, I couldn't imagine Jack altering his technique.

I felt so exposed that he'd pointed out I was starving part of my sex drive, I wanted to disappear. But I was transfixed by the way his hands moved as he massaged Jamie's feet. It reminded me of how he'd watched me rub the soles of my own feet to ease the labor contractions. Did he know what he was doing to me? When he reached across the table to pick Jamie up and his hand gently brushed against mine, a bolt flew through me and I pulled back. My pulse jumped, breath quickened, knees weakened. *Another accident*, I told myself. When I looked at him, I melted inside.

"I need to listen to Jamie's heart," he said at the end of the appointment. "It's easier if you hold her." He pulled the stethoscope from around his neck.

I stood before him, and he came in close to listen. My shoulder touched his chest, as he put the stethoscope on my baby's back and chest. I could have stayed in that moment for eternity. It calmed my senses. Standing with him like that, I breathed slowly into him. Warmth spread through my veins, and I felt the way I felt after sex with Jack—bonded.

One day a week, my mother-in-law, Candice, took the bus up from Boston to visit. I picked her up at the bus station in my Ford Explorer. Having Candice around helped me feel less isolated but intensified my feelings of inadequacy. My mother-in-law was an early-childhood expert and a saintly figure of self-denial. I was always behind on the learning curve. I read every book I could find about parenting and motherhood, trying to play catch-up. When I mastered one phase, Jamie was already starting the next stage. I wanted desperately to be a good mother, and I felt like everyone expected it to come effortlessly.

I also worried about my baby because she wasn't gaining weight. Dr. Richard wanted appointments every other week. I also worried that I would act out with Dr. Richard and behave inappropriately, so I started to plan my physician appointments when Candice could chaperone. Then I had to go every week in July.

It was really hard going into those appointments week after week after week. I struggled to understand my feelings, my memory, and a growing feeling of isolation wrapping itself around me. I couldn't connect with people unless I was talking about the birthgasm. It was all I could think about. I remembered the way it felt feeling his fingers on my clit, back and forth. I wanted to know his touch. To feel it. I craved him and his contact.

I would sit and daydream, wondering what the heck had happened. I held my baby next to me and stared out the window and watched the birds at the birdfeeder. I took long walks with my baby. And I tried to breastfeed her all the time, but Jamie didn't like to eat. I worried that something was wrong with my breast milk. I worried that my anxiety about Dr. Richard put stress chemicals in my milk and gave my daughter an upset stomach. Then I felt guilty for thinking about Dr. Richard.

Yet it seemed almost natural to focus on a nice person who cared for my baby and me. Jack denied my emotions and the memory of the physician's touch. My thoughts of Dr. Richard became a powerful type of magic. The thought of him loving me enabled me to escape my reality. It released me from feeling judged by Candice and unloved by Jack. The more often I used these thoughts, the more entrenched the thinking became. And even when I was with my friends from class, other moms and their babies, or groups I volunteered with, I found the moments of isolation would move in and surround me, pulling me into their grip. It could happen anywhere, anytime. It happened when I had thoughts that I couldn't share, because I thought the recipient wouldn't accept the role of listener.

There were also times Jack reminded me that Dr. Richard didn't want me, as he turned his deaf ears on me. I withdrew from Jack; our marriage was dying, and part of me was starved for love. A glimmer of hope deep inside me fed me in those moments. My hope was the thought of being loved.

Losing Touch

In the summer of 2005, I started to lose touch with reality. What I didn't realize was that my perception was off, in subtle ways at first. I started having memories I couldn't confirm. Strange things started happening around the house that I couldn't explain. Plus, my skin was hot all over. The hot skin was a symptom of things to come. Every time I got sick, it was preceded by this prodromal skin sensation that I could describe only as "burning."

I was also more emotionally honest with myself than I had felt my entire life. When Jack denied my emotions in my postpartum haze, I felt things I could not deny. Jack was looking for something specific. He wanted me to play a role that was limited in expression. He wanted a subservient wife, like you see in old movies, to bring him a martini at the end of the workday. This was the wrong space for me. I needed a man to explore my way out of that memory of the physician. I needed a quest to overcome the memory, and to find something that could bring me deeper pleasure than I'd ever known before. Jack didn't want that role. He didn't want me to talk about Dr. Richard and my memory of being touched.

Instead, Jack reached to grab my ass. I shook him off and closed myself in the nursery with Jamie for the weekend. I cried and tried to plan a way out from Jack. I snuck out to the deck to call my sister, Chloe. When I explained my feelings to her, she was worried about me.

"Jack will be such an ass as an ex-husband," she said. "I mean, he's barely civil as it is now. How will he behave when he has no control?"

"I don't know." I paused, weighing the pros and cons of trying to leave. "I wish he was willing to help me. I feel so confused. Part of me wants to believe that Dr. Richard loves me, but I don't know. I mean, he's a stranger—I don't know him." I paused again, staring into the forest at the side of the deck, where I looked for him. "Do you believe in love at first sight?" I asked.

"Oh, I don't know. Not that I don't like your story about the wrong-number calls, but you really think he'd risk his career to contact you like that?" she asked. "I mean, it's just weird. Normally when someone is interested, they tell you directly."

"I know. It can't be real. I just don't know how to forget what happened," I said.

After I made my first resolution to leave Jack, I moved a twin bed into the nursery and stopped sleeping in the master bedroom. By the Monday of the next week, Jamie wasn't eating unless I was walking.

Tuesday afternoon, I went to clean the cat box. When I opened the cabinet under the sink, I noticed urine in the base of the replacement tray. There was no apparent spillage on either side, and the odor was not as strong as cat urine typically is. Did "urine" mean "near you"? Was it a game? *Didn't he ask at the last visit, "Have you seen urine?"* It had thrown me off, but I hadn't really thought anything of it at the time. Or did it mean "you're in"? *That is too bizarre. It has to be the cats.* I locked all the windows and doors, then picked up the phone.

"At the last visit with Dr. Richard, did he say anything about urine?" I asked Candice.

"Why? Is everything all right with Jamie?" she asked, out of concern for her only grandchild.

"I think so. There's just so much to pay attention to at the visits. I was trying to remember what he said." I walked a slow lap around the kitchen, living room, and dining room as we talked on the cordless phone.

"Well, let's see. We got there and the nurses had us check her weight, and he was concerned about her weight, but I don't think he said anything about her urine. Maybe he said to make sure she is getting enough breast milk and supplementation with formula, we should check for urine," Candice said, seeming to add and emphasize the concern about the weight gain, thus adding to my insecurity.

"I just don't remember, but thanks for going with me. There's another visit next week. Are you able to make it?" I asked hopefully.

"I think so, but there's a meeting that I will miss," she said.

I thought back to the appointment when Dr. Richard had asked me if I'd seen urine. "What are you talking about?" I asked him.

If Candice was right, and he didn't say it as I remembered it, when would that appointment where the memory had come from have happened? I went back to my notebooks and searched the pages documenting each visit. There wasn't an appointment I had gone to alone since the postpartum visit. It was impossible.

He was already married, and so was I. I tried to forbid myself to think of him, but I kept getting calls for "Karen." The calls even found me in Kansas, where Jamie and I had flown to visit family, when my mom received a wrong-number call for Karen. There was stale urine under the sink again when we got home to New Hampshire.

Instead of him, I tried to imagine a fictitious character who would be near me: I called him Emraen. Emraen was free to love me. In my fantasy world, I wrote about Dr. Emraen and me in response to the phone calls and messages made up of the anagrams—sentences and words with special messages just for me when they were read backward. I needed a sense of control over my thoughts, and the only way I could control my environment was with creative play and fantasy. It was exhausting trying to harness my desire, and I had Jamie to care for. The constant little reminders took me too far. I didn't know how to cope.

I imagined what it would be like to touch Emraen and be with him. I wanted to know if it would feel as incredible as I imagined it to be. Just to be near him. I'd spend entire walks dreaming. I listened to "Linger," by the Cranberries, over and over with my earphones. I wrote down everything I was experiencing.

One Sunday in early August, Jack's mom and her friend came to visit. Jack and I left Jamie with them as they tried to feed her. We went out in the canoe and floated by the wetlands in Little Turkey Pond in Concord. The red-winged blackbirds called out over the water, and the large blue dragonflies flirted with the skirt of the canoe.

"There's something I have to tell you," I said.

"What is it?" Jack asked, glancing across the canoe at me.

"I'm afraid," I said, and looked intently over the hull at him. "Things have been happening that I can't explain."

He looked at me curiously.

"Huh?" He squished his face, not sure what I was talking about.

"The wrong-number calls. They keep happening. I'm afraid," I said.

"It is just the phone company. Somebody gave out the wrong number. It's okay," he said.

"But that isn't all of it." I took a deep breath and decided to tell him everything. "Remember that girls' night out that I went to? Where I met two women who had recently lost husbands? I don't think it was a coincidence. I think there may be something serious going on, and I'm scared. Remember how the other day I forgot and left the window open downstairs? Well, I'm afraid someone is sneaking into the house and leaving urine."

"The cats have been misbehaving ever since Jamie was born," he said.

"You don't understand. This is scary. I think there is a plot to harm you. I am worried that you'll be killed, like those two women's husbands were, on the roads of New Hampshire." Tears stained my cheeks.

He stopped when he saw my concern. He swallowed hard, looking bewildered.

A plane glided above the pond.

"Are they trying to find us?" I asked, terrified of the plane above. I told him enough to make him very worried.

"I think we need to go home," he said.

That evening, I called a friend. I told her everything I'd told Jack. The friend had hosted the party and knew what I was talking about. That friend was the only person who could give an unbiased perspective on my theory.

"Sweetheart, you need to see a psychiatrist. You are having postpartum psychosis. None of this is true. Those deaths were accidents. It was a coincidence. Please make an appointment to see a doctor as soon as you can." It was already 9:00 p.m. when I got off the phone—too late to see a psychiatrist.

When my friend told me I was sick, I trusted her. When she labeled my condition as psychotic, it was then that I knew that things weren't right. I struggled with what was real and what wasn't real. I needed perspective to help me gain insight into losing touch. The little constant messages and reminders made me paranoid. I connected the dots when no connection anybody would believe existed. I theorized there must be a conspiracy to inflate the number of deaths on the New Hampshire roads by killing people. I worried for Jack, because of his legislative agenda. He supported the NRA and the Second Amendment Foundation. It was the first time anybody had told me that I'd lost touch with reality.

Single Black Glove

The next day, I was walking laps with my baby around the house when I saw a single, black fleece glove placed on the arm of the sofa. I was home alone. How had it gotten there? It had appeared between one of the laps. I quickened my pace past the sofa, through the dining room, holding Jamie tight.

Was someone there?

My mind was ablaze with thoughts. In the O. J. Simpson trial, the key piece of evidence for the defense was the black glove found at the scene. I'd read the theory that one of the jury members believed in God and had heard a sermon about missing socks being evidence of a God. The idea was that God had interfered in the O.J. case; according to the article, the single black leather glove was God's mark.

Is somebody gonna come and kill me?

Why the hell *is there a black glove on the sofa?*

How did it get there?

I looked at the sofa, then turned back and walked through the kitchen. The lap took less than five seconds. A brief moment in time. The cats were nowhere to be seen.

How did the glove land on the armrest of the sofa?

Considering the options terrified me.

Who could have snuck in so fast? Is there a stalker in the house? Maybe this is an act of God. Or is it time travelers? I hoped it was the cats, but how could they have done it without my seeing them? Did I have selective vision?

I raced to the stairs. I held Jamie tight and rushed to lock myself and my baby in the nursery. I rocked her in my arms and cried. In my darkest moments of terror, locked in the nursery, holding Jamie in my arms, I prayed to God for protection from the terror of isolation in my country house and the thought of the single black glove.

Tears stained my face as I recited Psalm 23, a prayer I'd learned as a young child to deal with darkness when my parents turned off the lights. I relied on the teachings of my childhood that God is good. I didn't know how else to deal with the fear and terror of my experience. When things started happening that I couldn't explain, my basic instincts led me to trust in God.

> *The Lord is my shepherd; I shall not want. . . .*
> *Yea, though I walk through the valley of the shadow of death,*
> *I will fear no evil, for thou art with me;*
> *Thy rod and thy staff, they comfort me.*

When Jack got home, he found me locked in the nursery, still holding Jamie in my arms, distraught.

"What is wrong?" he asked.

"Jack, I'm so afraid. Please stay with me," I said.

"What happened?" he asked.

"I was home alone; then a single black glove appeared on the sofa, and I don't know how it got there," I said.

"I'm sure it was the cats," he said, unable to connect beyond conversation as I rocked Jamie gently.

I never knew fear like I did that summer I first lost my mind. Jack didn't understand but realized by then that something was seriously wrong.

That night, Jamie and I moved back into the master bedroom. I was still afraid, and by morning I'd barely slept. My mind was racing.

"Please don't leave me home alone," I begged Jack when he woke up.

"What do you want me to do? I need to work," he said.

"I'm too afraid to keep going on like this. I need help. My friend said I should see a psychiatrist. I need help finding one. I'm afraid to talk on the phone. I don't think I can tell someone what's going on without crying," I said, feeling tears threaten my eyes.

"Okay, today I'll stay home and look up providers, but you need to understand it's all in your head. The glove was just the cats. I don't understand why you're making such a big deal out of this. It seems pretty simple to me," he said.

He called everyone on the insurance company's website until we found Dr. Bouley, whose office had an opening the next day. We made an appointment.

Dr. Bouley, a gentle older man, saw me right away when I arrived at his office.

"Tell me why you are here today," he said.

"Well, I wouldn't have come, but I'm afraid, and my friend thinks I have postpartum psychosis." He waited for me to explain what that meant to me.

"She said I was delusional. I told her about the conspiracy to kill abusive husbands, and I'm afraid they will harm Jack. I'm so afraid," I said.

He cut me off and asked, "Yes, well, how are you sleeping?"

"Not well. Maybe a few hours here and there." I felt exhausted.

"Are you experiencing any other symptoms? Hearing or seeing things?" he asked.

"Well, there are the images of people who visit me in the nursery," I said. It hadn't occurred to me that this wasn't normal until he asked about it. I had talked to Jack's dad's spirit when he passed in 2000. But I had never dared tell Jack, because I knew it would upset him.

"How do you know they are images, and not real?" he asked.

"They look like auras. They are not natural-looking. They have a light green ring around the outline of the shape. Not really a fully formed person," I said.

"Hmmm. It may be a form of a visual migraine, or a seizure of some type. You need to see a neurologist, and we need to test your thyroid levels, and I want you to have a CT scan. It sounds like you are able to encapsulate these symptoms, but there are medications that may help you feel not so afraid," he said. "Tell me what else has you concerned."

"I'm afraid someone is breaking into the house, moving things around, and marking territory with urine. It's their way of telling me I'm in. 'You're in.' Get it—'urine'? I think it's part of a conspiracy. But my husband tells me it's our cats behaving badly."

"Are you involved in this plot?" he asked.

"No, I'm terrified of it," I said. Tears filled my eyes.

"I want you to come back in two days. Okay? Call if anything gets worse." He passed me the tissue box. He immediately started to write me prescriptions for the antipsychotic medication Seroquel and for Ambien sleeping pills.

"There's something else I need to tell you." I paused and carefully considered my choice of words. "While I was in labor, there was something that happened during an examination. I was touched intimately during an exam to check my progress in labor. I found labor pleasurable—every contraction felt identical to the orgasmic contractions I had during pregnancy—but now I feel haunted by the touch of Dr. Richard, and I don't know what happened anymore. Between fantasy and reality, I can't stop thinking about it."

"Memories are a complex thing," he said.

"How do I know if it was real?" I asked.

"Time heals the memory," he reassured me. I leaned forward in the chair and held on to his words, praying that he was right. I wanted to be better.

I went home, took the medication Dr. Bouley prescribed, and fell asleep. I slept for the first time in weeks. Jack had called my mom to tell her what was happening, and she arrived the next day. It was her second visit to New Hampshire since Jamie was born. I could barely walk down the stairs to greet her. My limbs were heavy and dull. My mind was in a thick fog. My eyes squinted against the lights. We hugged, and she cried at the sight of me, knowing from Jack what was going on in my mind.

"I need rest," I said. She nodded, and I turned back up the stairs and shuffled back to bed. I alternated between sleep, visions, and my emotional responses to what I was experiencing.

I went in to see Dr. Bouley two days later.

"How are you?" he asked me after I settled into the chair.

"I still see things, spirits are visiting, and I get scared," I said.

At this second visit, Dr. Bouley prescribed Geodon, another anti-psychotic. Geodon was fine, other than the akathisia (a feeling of restlessness), sedation, and the inability to concentrate it caused. But I was still on the break between summer session and the fall semester of classes.

When I saw Dr. Bouley again, I sat in the chair and he looked me over.

"How are you?" he asked.

"At least I'm sleeping well since I saw you last week, now that I have medication. I'm not afraid now. I can leave the nursery at night without terror when it is my turn to feed Jamie. Also, I haven't seen as many of the spirits visit me. But I still feel the conspiracy, and there are still the wrong-number calls," I said.

"How do you feel physically?" he asked me.

"This medication makes me feel like my body is strung out. I feel like time is moving in slow motion, and I'm sleepy," I said.

"Well, you will grow stronger and less sedated as you build up a tolerance to the side effects," he said.

On the car ride home after the appointment, my mom drove. "I'm worried about what you will do when I go," she said.

"Mom, we can hire a nursing assistant to help out. We can afford it. I just have to make it a priority with Jack," I said.

"But I'm worried about you," she said. I could hear her voice wavering as she spoke.

"Mom, I can't deal with your emotions about this when I'm still processing my own."

Mom stopped with the probing questions but continued to call the psychiatrist and try to get information from him once she returned home to Kansas City. When I had my routine appointment with Dr. Bouley, he brought it up.

"Before we get started, there is something we need to discuss," Dr. Bouley said. "About your mother: she has been calling repeatedly and would like information, but you have to approve it. She is very concerned about your well-being."

"I don't answer her calls, because she is too worried, and it stresses me out and makes me feel bad about myself. She doesn't have accurate information to share with you about my health. I do not want her to have access," I said.

"Are you sure? She cares a lot about you, and I think it would make her feel better," he said.

"I can't have her calling you, saying she thinks I'm psychotic, every time I don't want to talk to her," I stated.

"Hmm, well, that would be a problem," he said.

"I just wish she had hope for me and believed that the medication will allow me to lead a healthy, happy life, but right now I'm struggling to believe it, and the stigma really hurts," I said.

"Stigma?" he asked.

"Well, I was at the moms' group meeting last week, and I shared about what I'm going through with seeing things. A group of moms turned their backs to me at the end of the meeting, effectively shunning me," I said.

When he saw the tears in my eyes, Dr. Bouley handed me tissues. He referred me to a social worker, Harrison, who could help me deal with my illness. This was one of the best things he could have done for me: to give me my own advocate who could train me how to cope with my issue.

On the first visit to Harrison's office in downtown Manchester, I rolled off the elevator with Jamie in the Jeep stroller. The country-green diaper bag was tucked in the undercarriage, and we strolled down the corridor to the small office waiting room. I walked in and read the sign: NEW PATIENTS, PLEASE FILL OUT THESE FORMS. I took the clipboard and started filling in the blanks. Jamie got bored as soon as I sat down, so I took her out of the carriage and held her at my hip, trying to fill out the form.

My anxiety had motivated me to leave far too early for the appointment. It was a bright, sunny day, the reception area was deserted, and I wondered if I was in the right location. I looked around at the art on the pale walls and the dark green painted trim. A painting of laundry hanging on a line was humorous to me, as Harrison was a social worker and marriage therapist. There was also a copy of the

American Medical Association's *Code of Medical Ethics* on the coffee table, along with every issue of the *New Yorker* from the past four years.

By the time Harrison poked his head between the door and the frame, looking into the waiting room to check on us, I had filled out the paperwork. Jamie kept fussing, even though I tried to entertain her. When his previous patient departed, he waited a few moments, then invited us into his spacious office.

"So tell me, why are you here?" Harrison asked.

I explained that I thought I had postpartum psychosis and told him about my experience with stigmatization by the moms' group.

He responded quickly. "Are you familiar with depression?" he asked.

"I guess I am. Why?" I asked.

"Well, everything you described fits the *DSM*'s diagnosis criteria for depression," he stated.

"Really?" I asked.

"Yes," he said. "I'll even show you the book." He walked over to the bookshelf, grabbed the four-inch-thick diagnostic manual for mental health professionals, and walked back to the sofa, flipping through the pages. "Here it is," he said, pointing to the entry. "I'm going to make you a copy so you can look at it and reflect on it later." He walked back to his copier and printed a single sheet for me.

Harrison said people would be able to understand better if I called it depression. I didn't understand it better, so I kept writing in my journal and took the Geodon, Ambien, and Ativan. I also started to study up. I wanted to know what to expect from my illness.

My difficulty concentrating had me on edge, but by the end of the month, I had read every book I could find about mental illness. One of them, which a friend recommended, made me doubt the medical model and modern psychiatry. It was the book *Mad in America*.

The psychiatrist had recommended that I not change a thing and that I continue seeing Dr. Richard. I didn't understand Dr. Bouley's logic, and Jack refused to allow me to go for Jamie's well-child checkup

without him. It caused me great anxiety and unhappiness to have to
see Dr. Richard. Reality reminded me how sick I was. When I looked
into Dr. Richard's eyes, I felt so sad.

"How are you doing?" he asked.

"I take the medication every day, but my memories haven't gone
away," I said.

Dr. Richard knew about the antipsychotics. When I'd started the
medication, I'd signed a written release giving my providers permission to communicate about my case. My mother was concerned that I
shouldn't breastfeed, so she called Dr. Richard. He responded immediately to my mom that it was contraindicated to breastfeed while
taking any antipsychotics. Dr. Bouley told me that he'd gotten a call
from Dr. Richard about the breastfeeding issue.

After Dr. Richard talked to my mom, she wouldn't let me breastfeed again. My milk dried up within a few weeks. It made me even
sadder when I stopped breastfeeding. I still held Jamie in a sling most
hours of the day and fed her with a bottle whenever she would accept
food.

Dr. Richard sat behind the small computer desk in the operatory.
Jack was glaring at him from the chair at the side of the room. Tears
welled up in my eyes, and I swallowed them back. I hadn't slept for
days. The psychiatrist had to prescribe more sleeping medication and
tranquilizers for me to deal with the situation.

"You know you don't have to go back to Dr. Richard," Chloe said.

I finally decided to change primary care providers. I called and
made an appointment for an annual physical with another physician.
It was the right thing to change doctors. When the afternoon came,
my burning skin was terrible, so I decided to do something to try to
make it go away. I posted a new profile on AdultFriendFinder.com.
I alternated between reality and fantasy. I hoped to find Dr. Richard
this way. I believed if he loved me, we would find a way to communicate. I searched and searched for him, and that helped my feelings
of desperate isolation go away. It was the best I'd felt in a long time.
I was in deep psychological pain from the memory of Dr. Richard's
touch, yet I craved the physiologic rush of the memory. I'd become
a junkie for the memory of his touch. I tried to juxtapose my own

desire with the knowledge that my experience was clinical and he didn't actually want me. The only thing that made me feel better was to talk about it, and the only safe place I could share was in my secret online world as Sunny, with my fictitious lover, Emraen. It helped me feel like I had some control over my thoughts. I started chatting with a Richard M., whom I met online, because I couldn't talk about what had happened to me without upsetting my family.

I told Harrison and the psychiatrist about my online correspondence. I knew they didn't think it was helpful, but I couldn't stop. I needed to write. Writing acted as a temporary salve for my pain. Richard M. and others put up with my desire for Dr. Richard, hoping for something more. Jack knew I'd met some people online through Adult Friend Finder, and it upset him. I kept trying not to e-mail, but I needed an outlet for what was going on inside my mind, because Jack wouldn't listen to or work through it with me. I couldn't talk about my desire for Dr. Richard with Harrison or Dr. Bouley, because it made them uncomfortable.

"Imagine a probe being inserted into your brain," Harrison would say when he wanted me to change my thinking.

I got the probe-in-the-brain metaphor every time I brought up my feelings for Dr. Richard. It didn't help. I kept promising Jack that I would stop the correspondence.

Dr. Bouley prescribed something for my anxiety. He said my delusions about all the different conspiracies would go away, and they did, with the exception of my issue about being touched during Jamie's birth and the encounters with Dr. Richard.

I asked Jack if he was okay with my going on adult websites. He wasn't, so I deleted my posts. I was rude to my pen pal, and he went away.

The thought of failing out of graduate school scared me even more than my symptoms. The side effects of akathisia and a lack of concentration were too much to take. Geodon was not comfortable for me. I hated the feedback from my body about that medication, which left me with a pulling sensation that the medical literature called "inner restlessness"; I hated the feeling of being strung out. The only thing that helped to clear out the clouded fog in my thinking was cigarettes, which I snuck with a few of my mommy friends. Then I discovered eating eased the pain and pulling feeling in my body. I couldn't stop eating graham crackers. After a few months, I decided it was too uncomfortable. I had forgotten to take my medication for a day, and on the second day I decided I just couldn't take it anymore. I went off the antipsychotic meds cold turkey. I got the shakes and survived on hot tea. Hell.

I told my psychiatrist about my decision to stop the antipsychotic medications at my weekly visit. He told me I was lucky to have survived my sudden withdrawal from the antipsychotics; he said going off drugs the way I did can be fatal. He recommended I keep our visits going, to check in about my anxiety and sleep difficulties, and I agreed.

My burning skin also subsided with anxiety medication, but I still felt it a little. When I was on the tranquilizers, the sensation was still there, but the medication changed the feeling. I didn't mind feeling my skin on sedatives. However, I could see people's energy auras.

Somehow, I managed to make it through my coursework, take care of Jamie, and more. When I was working, I arranged child care with a community-based co-op behind the local strip mall, and with Jack's mom. I volunteered in the moms' club and at the co-op, nonprofits, and coalitions. I could function in these groups as long as I didn't open up about my mental illness and invite stigmatization. When I did allude to my struggles, I referred to them as "postpartum depression." Six months earlier, Tom Cruise had criticized Brooke Shields for seeking therapy and taking antidepressants. When the public defended Shields's decision to treat her postpartum depression, I felt a sense of community support. I read her story in the book *Down Came the Rain* cover to cover and found that similar feeling of recognition I felt when I read Elyn R. Saks's book *The Center Cannot Hold: My Journey Through Madness*.

I would sit on the bench at the co-op, reading books to children, trying to stay in the moment, but as soon as the toddlers and preschoolers moved on to the next activity, my mind would return to trying to solve the pieces of my broken puzzle. The birthgasm had changed me, and I was trying to understand what had happened by going back to look at the pieces of my story. The only thing I truly knew was that an exam happened, I had a baby, and my mind kept replaying the vivid memory of the experience.

While my emotional path to recover from the memory progressed slowly, my academic rebound was swift. Since I'd quit the antipsychotic, I was taking only the sleeping and anxiety medications. I participated in class, contributed to projects, and could study well. My academic performance was my greatest strength. Focusing on graduate coursework gave me hope for a future that wasn't delusional. I had the grades to prove it.

I was doing so well in school in the spring of 2006, I would graduate on time with my class. I had served as a president of an organization and volunteered with the policy committee of another. I'd even been invited to run for the board of directors of that association.

I wrote up my campaign bio in February, and the ballot with my bio in it came in the mail in March. It was early April when they reported the final tally. I got an e-mail telling me that I'd lost by one vote. At first I joked that I felt like Al Gore in 2000, but not to worry, because I didn't want a recount. The group I e-mailed sent replies that they voted for Al Gore, too. Later that month, I would get an e-mail from the board saying that by a unanimous vote, they'd appointed me to fill a vacant board seat for the coming year. But it was too late— my thinking had already slipped by then.

Welcome to Myspace

At the end of March 2006, I discovered Myspace. I learned about the new site when an e-mail was sent to a "Marissa" with a user name (my e-mail address) and a password (sammyjr3). When I got the e-mail, I became paranoid. Who had sent it? I had not created the account myself. The only possibility I wanted to think of was that Dr. Richard had set it up so that he could have another way of sending me secret messages. Or had someone else set it up?

"Jack, I think there's an account for some Myspace thing that was created in my name," I said to him. "I think my e-mail was hacked."

Jack seemed annoyed, but he opened up his laptop and surfed the Internet for a few minutes, sleuthing around to figure out if my story checked out.

"Looks like Myspace has terrible security," he concluded. "Change your password."

He was an information security professional, so I trusted he knew better than I did, and I changed all my passwords. But I started to think about the password on the account. Sammyjr3. I read it backward. Why "mas"? Using my training in Spanish I translated "mas" to "more." "Why more?" The answer to the question "Why mas?" was "Sammy." I cried for the loss of hope that I would have a baby boy one day. Sammy was the name I'd picked for a son. I'd told only a few people; mostly the name was a secret because Jack and I didn't want to hear others' opinions on the subject. "Jr" meant I would have grandchildren by my son, Sammy. Three was my lucky number. I kept that e-mail on file.

For the first few days, I wondered about the new Myspace account.

Had it really been randomly generated? Had someone I knew created the account? It upset me. I wanted it to be Dr. Richard, but what if it had been someone else? Before I'd gotten sick, I'd wanted to someday have another child, and I still wanted that under ideal circumstances, but at present, knowing how sick I was made doing that feel wrong. I didn't even know whether it was safe to have children if I took antipsychotic medication. I didn't want to risk having a child who suffered because of my treatments for my illness.

In response to my new account, I did the same thing someone had done to me: I opened an account linked to the e-mail for Dr. Richard, and I started to write. I had found Dr. Richard's personal e-mail account during a Google search on April Fool's Day. I took a photo I had of him and selected only a thin band to show his eyes with glasses on for the profile. I wrote personal blog entries under Dr. Richard's account. I wrote about my life, how I felt, but mostly I wrote about how much I desired him. I also posted stories and the beginnings of romance novels I'd written.

The username belonged to Dr. Richard, but we both knew the password "NotEnough?" because the security on Myspace was so terrible that it e-mailed the password to the address the user signed up with. There was no account verification feature. I took advantage of it as a way to communicate secretly with Dr. Richard.

For years I had been keeping notebooks that contained my personal writing and various lists that I created. Shortly after I received the e-mail about the Myspace account, I began looking over some of my writing and seeing certain marks—such as highlighting and underlining—that I didn't recall having put there myself.

Once I started seeing these signs beyond the telephone, in my house, and in my notebooks, I saw signs everywhere. Even license plates held special meaning. At first it was just the plates I saw when out on my walk, but soon I couldn't stop seeing meaning in everything. These messages appeared as anagrams.

I wanted to tell someone about what I was seeing, and the first person I thought of sharing it with was Jack, but our communication was worse than ever. He'd gone back to shooting on a pistol team and spent most of his time in the basement, reloading ammo for the team's meets. That often left me alone in the living room, where one night I decided to e-mail Dr. Richard. I sent him the first scene of an erotic story in which I imagined meeting him at a conference. I wanted to seduce him with my writing.

In another e-mail, I asked Dr. Richard if I should call my psychiatrist because I was seeing signs.

First thing Monday morning, the phone rang. "Is Sunny there?" a woman's voice asked.

"This is she," I replied.

"This is your primary care provider, and I heard from Dr. Richard that you have been e-mailing him. He won't share the e-mails, but you have him concerned. I think you need to make an appointment to see your psychiatrist," my new primary care physician said.

"I have an appointment Friday," I said.

"Are you seeing signs?" she asked.

"Well, yes," I admitted hesitantly.

"What are you seeing?" she asked.

"Well, I see things in license plates. I think the messages are for me. And when I read my personal writing, some of it has great meaning to me."

"I would appreciate it if you would tell me about its meaning," she said kindly.

"It is deeply symbolic for me." Everything I wrote in my large red notebook symbolized what I believed was magic from another world. In fact, everything I read, saw, heard, and spoke had special meaning to me. As I listened to Madonna singing "Like a Virgin" in the background on the stereo, it all made sense. It gave me the idea that I might be like Madonna, Jesus's mother. Had I given birth to God's child? Only I was not "like a virgin."

"I'm not sure what is real and what isn't," I told the doctor.

"To be on the safe side, I think you should call and move up the appointment," she responded.

"Okay, I will. Thanks for calling. I will call Dr. Bouley now," I said. I immediately called him and made the next available appointment.

On Tuesday, I went to see Dr. Bouley. I had my daughter and her large Jeep stroller with me. No one would ever have guessed what was happening in my mind. We were clean and looked like we'd stepped fresh from the pages of *Parents* magazine when we presented ourselves at the psychiatrist's office.

I told him about the e-mails to Dr. Richard, and the signs. "I believe that God has a plan and I'm part of it," I told him.

"Here, you need to be taking these. You are experiencing psychosis," he said gently but firmly, handing me samples and a prescription to fill for Geodon, the same antipsychotic medication I had taken in the fall.

I trusted Dr. Bouley, so I decided to comply with his instructions. I nodded and opened my hand, where he placed the medication. I stopped at a Dunkin' Donuts near the hospital, and while I waited in line, I listened carefully to the words on the radio. As I realized how powerless I felt against the messages surrounding me, I knew I had to resign myself to letting go of my ego. *Here we go again*, I thought. I ordered a large iced coffee and took my medication with it before Jamie and I did anything else.

It was midafternoon when I left the drive-through line. I spent the afternoon walking along the Merrimack River by the Manchester campus and playing on a blanket in the grassy patch near the sidewalk next to the water on the east side of the river. About an hour later, despite my iced coffee, I started to feel sedated. Jamie descended into a fussy, miserable mess by 4:00 p.m.—the "witching hour," as Jack's mom called it. I tried everything, but she refused food, comfort, and entertainment. The only thing I could do to pacify her was to carry her around in my arms and walk. But that afternoon, I was too tired from the medicine, so we went back to the car. As Jamie crawled into my lap, crying, my eyelids and limbs became heavier and heavier, and I eventually succumbed to the sensation.

I woke from my deep sedation to the sound of tapping on the tinted window. It was a police officer. He wore a blue uniform with a shiny new badge on his chest. His skin was dark brown. I opened the door, smiling slightly.

"May I see your identification, Officer?" I asked.

"Yes, here it is," he said, holding up an identification badge. "We got a call about an unattended child in a green SUV." My face burned with the heat of a blush as he told me why he was there. He looked at me with my child in my lap. "But there must have been a misunderstanding, because everything looks fine," he said. "Can I close the back gate on the trunk?"

"Sure, it was too heavy for me to close earlier," I said. He looked like he felt bad for us as my daughter continued to fuss and I held her, trying to bounce and pat her to quiet her down in front of the officer. Jamie was still miserable, and I was still struggling against the sedation, but we looked perfectly ordinary, other than my delayed responses and Jamie's tearstained cheeks.

Jack got to the Manchester campus parking lot that afternoon and took Jamie home. I didn't talk to him immediately about the police officer incident or my appointment with Dr. Bouley. It wasn't that I hid it; it just didn't occur to me that I needed to tell him. After all, we rarely talked about anything anymore, since everything that came out of my mouth seemed to cause Jack to bristle.

Somehow, I made it to class and home that night, and I wrote in my journal. After the police incident, I felt terrible. I knew I couldn't care for my daughter adequately if I was sedated. By Wednesday, April 19, 2006—only one day after the psychiatrist had prescribed me the Geodon—I decided to stop taking it. I'd become too sedated to take care of Jamie the day before, and hiring help hadn't occurred to me that day. The only thought I could focus on was taking care of my baby.

At noon that same day, I put Jamie in her gray high chair and sat down to eat lunch at the McDonald's in Concord, New Hampshire. Jamie perched across from me, facing Main Street, while my back was against a booth bench. There was an old man sitting in the corner booth next to us.

In my heightened awareness, I was seeing the signs in everything. Earlier, I'd seen a cloud that looked like a pie in the sky, so I wasn't surprised to see the next sign. Sitting with my back against the window, I read another customer's hat. The words were laced through the comical buttons pinned around the man's ball cap. He was into politics, and he supported a liberal presidential candidate, John Kerry. Sitting with Jamie, looking at the ball cap, I saw something special. The sporting gear told me I was near God. The man was a Bruins fan. I read an anagram in "Bruins": "S near B." "S" symbolized my name, Sunny, and I'd determined "B" meant "God." The bees were essential to nature, and that was God's domain. Plus, I was a terrible speller, so I sounded out "niur" to mean near. At the time it made sense to me; I read the anagram backward.

After I settled into the seat and got Jamie's meal organized, the old man next to us started talking. "I am a great-grandfather," he said.

"I hope to grow old enough to see my great-grandchildren," I said. "Isn't that what life is all about?" I smiled and relaxed, knowing I was safe with God nearby.

He just smiled back at me. We started talking about life and kids. When Jamie dropped her Happy Meal toy, a small boat with a bell that chimed every time the boat rocked, I felt the old man studying her as I went to pick up the plastic toy from the floor.

"It's like a ladder: when people start to fall off, you catch them and help them back up," he said. "How old is your daughter?"

"She's thirteen months," I said.

"I'm over eighty years old," he said.

"Oh, wow," I said. "What do you do for work?"

"I've been a baby farmer my whole life," he said with an appreciative look in his eye. We talked about parenthood for a while, until Jamie and I were done eating. I figured it made sense that God was a baby farmer. Every farmer I knew tried to do the best for his herd or crop, but sometimes the farmers I knew made hard choices about the animals they raised. It caused me to think about our world from a new perspective.

When I got home, I called my mom to tell her about my experience. "I think I ate lunch with God," I said.

My mom didn't believe it at all. "What are you talking about?" she asked.

"Well, Jamie and I ate lunch at McDonald's on Main Street in Concord, and I think I met God," I said.

"That's impossible," she said.

I felt like my mother was a stranger to me in that moment. My mother was a good Christian woman; if she didn't believe in experiencing God, then who would? I got off the phone as soon as I could.

When I read a message on the hat, as a real man sat at the table next to me, the experience explained the universe in ways I could understand. Society's role is to pick people up and help them get back on the ladder of life. The idea resonated with me in a deep way. I needed to hear that. I struggled to imagine a future living with mental illness, and thinking God was a baby farmer was the simplest explanation I'd ever heard for why I was living with an illness.

I reflected for a long time about how to frame my experience. The way I came to accept my "lunch with God" was that I was sick and I ate lunch with an old, possibly senile, man. He was probably struggling with mental health as much as or more than I was. But I needed to hear those things at that time. It helped me have hope for a future when I needed it most.

That evening, I felt like I was on fire. My skin was burning hot. Radiating.

Messages appeared in my inbox. The e-mails told me it was neuropsychiatric, exothermic, and a couple other things. I thought they were meant for me, but Jack said it was just spam and I wasn't that special. I thought someone was trying to tell me about my burning-skin condition. I got paranoid and erased many of the e-mails. I thought someone knew everything about me. I hoped it was Dr. Richard. To cope with my desire, fear, and paranoia, plus my worry about Jack and all the time he spent building firearms in the basement, I opened a file and documented my experience by writing passages such as the following:

Thursday, April 20, 2006
There is nowhere to go.
There is no one to turn to.
And I see a psychiatrist and a social worker; I sit in a public health classroom; I have coffee with moms, shop at the mall, go on picnics in the park and strolls through my neighborhood.

Why can't I talk to anyone?
Why am I isolated?
Okay, maybe not functioning totally normally.
After all, I thought I ate lunch with God.
Who would ever believe that?
My mother doesn't even seem to buy it at all.
And if she doesn't believe in it, then nobody would.

I am afraid of what the signs say.
I would never do anything like what they want me to do.
You picked the wrong person.

I would rather be poisoned to death than hurt anyone.
I could never live with the guilt of it.
Angels will have to rescue me from this living hell.
Angels, please come and rescue me.
Take me away.

I feel sad.
The house has a terrible smell.
It smells like sewer gases.
My husband told me he thought it smells like my perfume.
It does not smell anything like Chanel Chance.

After I finished writing, I decided I needed to say something to Jack about how suspicious I was of him. I walked into the kitchen, where he was sitting at a stool. He turned to look at me when I walked into the room. At first, there was a long pause, a tense silence. I was the first to break the quiet.

"I know your secret," I said.

He looked at me, still letting the silence fall.

"I know you have the explosives. I saw them. Why are you building a bomb?" I asked.

"What are you talking about?" Jack asked.

"How could you hide it in Jamie's room?" I asked. I watched his face blanch.

We quarreled about the basement and the reloading equipment and what I assumed to be an explosive in Jamie's room.

"You need medication—you're crazy!" he yelled at me. A wave of fatigue hit me, and I turned and retreated to bed.

The next morning, I felt a little better having had a good night's sleep, but Jack handed me the medication he'd found while searching my handbag. "You will take this, or I'll make sure you never see Jamie again," he warned. I complied in silence and felt him studying me as I swallowed the pills.

"I'm taking you to see Dr. Bouley today," he said.

In my moments of lucidity, I trusted my insight and the responses from the people around me, like when my mother didn't believe I ate lunch with God in McDonald's on Main Street. I fought my fear and listened when Jack told me he'd have Jamie taken away; I didn't doubt his threat. I knew he was serious that he would strip me of my rights as a mother if he could, and I resented him for that. I hated that he would use my love and need to mother Jamie to manipulate my behavior.

Afterward, Jack left with Jamie for the bus station, where he was picking up his mom, who planned to spend the day babysitting. I was upstairs doing my hair, when I heard a faint noise. I set down the brush and listened carefully.

"The farmer in the dell, the farmer in the dell, heigh ho the derry-o, the farmer in the dell." I could hear the creepy song playing across the landing as I went toward Jamie's room. I opened the door. One of Jamie's toys played from her crib. I didn't know what had activated it. The cats were nowhere in sight.

God said he was a farmer. Is he in the computer? It is a Dell.

When will I stop feeling afraid? Are they going to kill me? The only way I'll feel safe is if the FBI searches our house for bombs.

What I needed was protection. I was afraid Jack would follow through on his threat to take Jamie away from me, and I worried that there was a war between good and evil taking place over me.

Dr. Bouley had scheduled an appointment earlier in the week to reevaluate my condition that Friday. For the first time, Jack decided to accompany me. When we arrived, we encountered Dr. Bouley in the hall outside his office. He stopped short at the sight of Jack, whom he had never met, and peered at Jack over his eyeglass frames to inspect him from head to toe.

When we settled into his office, he sat in front of a beautiful, rich painting with a scarlet background and a light flower flowing across the canvas. I loved staring at the psychedelic piece when I visited him.

When we sat down, Dr. Bouley asked why Jack was there.

"I'm getting sicker," I said. "On Tuesday after our appointment, I took the medication. I was so sedated, I fell asleep in the parking lot and a police officer woke me up to the sound of a crying baby. My daughter was crying in my arms, and the trunk of the SUV was wide open. Someone must have heard her crying and called the police. I feel terrible, but I didn't think there was any other way to adjust to the medication. So I stopped taking it after that."

"I can send you home with more medication, and we could try ramping up the dose, like we did earlier in the week," Dr. Bouley said. I knew I wouldn't be able to care for my baby with that option. "Or you could be hospitalized and we could put you immediately on a therapeutic dose and monitor your adjustment in the hospital." I had needed that therapeutic dose three days earlier. If Dr. Bouley had seen my journal, he would have appreciated the seriousness of my condition. My family was not prepared to deal with my disease, and it would strain them to have me under their care the first time I totally lost my ability to encapsulate the disease, when the sands of morality and my ability to reason slipped from my grasp. That hospitalization was absolutely appropriate and necessary.

The thought of walking back to the car was too much to imagine. I felt powerless against what the messages were telling me. I felt controlled by something all-knowing. The thought of going to the Catholic Medical Center gave me hope. The perversion of thoughts in psychosis was too much to deal with alone. I needed support, and the pope as a spiritual leader gave me hope that I'd find safety from evil within the walls of one of his hospitals.

The sun was high in the sky on the brisk April morning when Jack drove me along the pine tree–lined roads of New Hampshire to the hospital.

My body felt heavy and sedated as the drive progressed. Jack and I had a tense silence going. I no longer trusted him in the basement. I knew I needed help, but I believed what the messages told me. It was too terrifying not to trust that whoever was in control would protect me. I was afraid to tell Jack what the car tags told me; it was more intense than God's being in my computer and seeing Him talk to me like that.

En route, I saw personalized license plates everywhere I looked. Every time I saw a plate, I read it backward phonetically. As the cars passed in front of us, the meaning in my world changed with each new tagline. I thought back to the message I saw driving near Manchester. The tag "Herin." The messages told me He was near and I was in. It also confirmed I was hearin' Him. My love for Dr. Richard was real. When I saw the messages, it felt like a drug being mainlined into my brain. It gave me a high.

At a certain point, instead of reading the signs, I looked down at the shoulder of the road. It was too much. As with the secret messages in the phone calls, I was pushed over the edge. The messages were no longer just coming from the phone; I saw them everywhere. I was florid with delusional thoughts.

Our Ford Explorer pulled up into the temporary parking lot down the block from the hospital, overlooking the Merrimack River. My limbs felt weighted down from the antipsychotic medication I'd been forced to take that morning. I could barely move, I felt so sedated, and the sunlight hurt my eyes. I stared out at the piles of junk metal the industrial equipment was sorting.

Even though my body dragged, I had pulled myself together that morning. I wore my favorite blue sweater, and my hair had started to get sun highlights from my spring walks with Jamie. Around my neck hung a papal coin, a crucifix, and a lotus flower with a butterfly landing on the petals.

We walked along the sloping sidewalk up to the hospital. When we got up to the psychiatric ward, Jack and I were taken into a patient intake room and interviewed by a nursing staff member. The nurse asked me why I was there.

"I'm having mental health issues," I said, and wrung my hands together at the table where I sat.

"What do you mean?" the nurse asked me.

"Well, would I be the first patient to tell you I felt safer being here because I feel like I'm under the pope's protection?" I asked.

"You wouldn't be the first." The nurse laughed. I smiled. "Will you tell me why you feel safer here because of the pope?"

"Well, it starts with this letter from my grandmother." I pulled out a slightly rumpled letter from my grandmother Ronan telling me that I needed to believe in Jesus in my time of need. "My name is Sunny Mera, and I think somebody more powerful than any of us is doing things to manipulate me. I see signs in everything: personalized license plates, billboards, even songs," I said, thinking back to that morning. "When I see things, I repeat them backward to find the secret messages." Then I pulled out the papal coin I had attached to my necklace. "I feel that there is power in this necklace. I think the pope is my only hope here on Earth to save me from what's happening."

The nurse reached out to touch my hand, and I looked up at her.

"What *is* happening?" she asked.

Tears welled up in my eyes. It was so hard to tell what was going on. "Well, it started with the beginning of spring," I said. "I want the pope to protect me. And I am concerned about Jack." I looked over at him. He knew my concern. I hadn't hidden any of my feelings from him. I looked back at the nurse and whispered, "I am afraid of my husband."

Jack clenched his jaw and turned from me.

The nurse looked at me, scrunching up her brows. She just sat there with us for a few seconds amid the emotional tension.

"Last night I went to sleep before I did anything. I didn't call the police or try knocking on the neighbor's door. I think it would have been hard to explain why I was knocking at midnight. I think the pope's protection is my only hope to save me from evil," I said.

I knew when the nurse leaned back in her chair that she didn't believe what I explained to be reality, but she looked back with sympathy. Then she took me away and left Jack in the waiting room. That was the last time I had to see Jack for a while.

When I got to the room, they were making the bed. As I watched them pull the sheets back from the bed, I saw the words "one love" at one end and my lucky number, 3, at the other. I thought it meant I was lucky in love. The view from the fourth floor was nice. The trees were starting to bud, and from my picture window I could see the church up the hill and the sunset behind it.

During my hospitalization, I worked on my graduate school coursework every second that I wasn't sleeping. The good thing about writing papers for policy debates was that I could check the facts and search the literature for references to support or argue against the issue.

The hospital room on the fourth floor held me for over a week. They gave me meds that I could concentrate with: Zyprexa. I produced good work—better than the average student's, anyway. I made As.

I kept a secret journal through the darkest days of my illness. I wrote on my laptop in between working on my research papers. I thought I was communicating with whoever was harassing me and trying to get me to love Dr. Richard.

In the Hospital
Friday, April 21, 2006
Here I am . . .
A day or two later since my last journal entry.
I've lost track of the days.
I have no sense of time.
I am afraid of my husband.
How can I return home?
My skin is burning.
I copied all the special e-mails into the keys doc.
My problem is that I didn't understand what I was supposed to do.
Nobody told me.

I hate you people who are part of this.
I think the person I saw tonight was not really my mother.
I hardly knew her. She was like a stranger to me.

Okay, I'm back.

I was thinking about the message I heard on the intercom/ PA system.

They called for one of my classmates.

You all are here.

At least I think you are.

In that case I am supposed to comply, and no worries, I will.

I just don't understand the messages.

You need to improve your communications!

I don't understand what you want from me.

Does it have something to do with the book about the hobos taking over the world?

The book recommended hiring professionals when you need an assassination.

I'm assuming you didn't really want me to do anything.

Hmmmmm.

I'm going to go find a dictionary and look up the messages you sent.

Half of the words are not in the dictionary.

Maybe the messages should be ignored. . . .

The messages I'm getting—what are they? Are they jumbled mixes of stories I've read from my web browser, and personal details from my life? How many people are reading this? Is anyone watching? Why do I feel like la femme Nikita, the CIA agent who is trained to live differently? When will this go away?

Maybe Jack is right. Maybe I am so crazy that I should feel lucky to have him take care of me. I feel worthless. I miss Jamie. I feel so sad that I am away from her. The worst part is that I feel like her grandmothers do a better job taking care of her than I do. I worry that I wasn't feeding her as well as I should have been. Was I unintentionally negligent?

You know you all have me with the paper trail.
If you go ahead and move on, then you will own me.
All the paper leads to me.
I think I am ready to trust you.
I just feel lucky to be alive.
Thank you.
And when this is over, I want to move on.
I want to get a job.
I am going to work.
And I want to get pregnant again.
I need to start over.
I'll start preparing for separation from my husband.
I'll get all my paperwork together.
I'll make a plan.
I don't know if I'll be able to function like my old self taking
these medications. I don't like the way my mouth feels.

Saturday, April 22, 2006
I see signs everywhere. They are all over the place. Everything
is connected through God. His tapestry of humankind is like
an anthill or a beehive.
I am so upset by the signs.

Tuesday, April 25, 2006
I don't know what just happened. I got a strange e-mail. It
simply stated "end," with a red background.

The last sign was in the driving directions for one of my continuing-education courses, where the final destination stated "end." The sign had much more meaning to me than just an e-mail. I considered the possibility that the sender was playing with me, but concluded that surely they wouldn't use their own e-mails to send subtle messages to a woman hospitalized in a psychiatric unit.

I can't believe I fell so in love with Dr. Richard. . . .
The only reason I'm not suicidal is the little note scribbled

at the foot of the bed: "one love," and my lucky number, 3, by
my head.

   I believe I was communicating with my spam e-mail.
   The problem was, it was too cryptic.

Thursday, April 27, 2006

They gave me a higher dose of medication.

   I am starting to feel like myself again. This is a good thing,
but I do feel a bit embarrassed. What will people think of me?
What does a person do when they experience something like
this?

   Sometimes if you don't laugh, you'll cry.

Friday, April 28, 2006

I'm in bed. A song is playing on the small Grundig radio.
Flowers are spread across the windowsill. I thought someone
was sneaking into the house and leaving signs everywhere. In
fact, I won't even write about what I really thought, because
what if it is true? Nobody would believe it. The delusions
snuck deep into my memory banks, leaving deposits on most
of the milestone events that happened in my life after Jamie's
conception.

   God, I trust you will care for me. I believe you sent your only
son, Jesus, to die for our sins, and I believe I am part of your
plan. I trust you will lead me on the right path.

Saturday, April 29, 2006

I hope God loves me enough to protect me. I am so in love
with Dr. Richard. I must believe in hope. My faith must be
strong for me to survive the rest of the semester.

By Monday in the hospital, my behavior was so good that they let
me out with the group to take walks when the social worker came in
to work. The group took a walk through the neighborhood near the
hospital. I recorded notes in my notebook on all the license plates I
saw, until someone asked me if I thought I was the meter maid or

something. I took the hint and suppressed my urge to document my surroundings.

Once I'd been in the hospital for a week, despite frequent visits from Jamie, I missed my baby, and my fear of Jack had eased, so I told my psychiatrist I was ready to go home. It was a voluntary hospitalization; I was not a threat to myself or others. We talked for a bit about my transition out of the hospital. I asked if there were day programs; I didn't want to be alone in my house anymore. He said he didn't know of any programs like that, but that I would see Harrison and him frequently, and all I had to do was call if I got worse and I needed to return to the hospital. But he thought I was responding well to the medication.

I survived the rest of the semester and made good grades. Emotionally, I was still starving for love, and the thought of Dr. Richard was still intoxicating, but I tried to stop the thoughts that he loved me—he was just doing his job.

It was all too much. At the heart of the dilemma was reconciling reality with the delusions. What was real? How would I manage to sift through the important aspects of reality?

May 22, 2006

I thought this happened because I fell in love with Dr. Richard. I was e-mailing his e-mail. I couldn't keep my thoughts to myself about him. He e-mailed me back from his e-mail. He said the correspondence was inappropriate and should stop. I stopped the posts on the Myspace account. I left it alone.

I thought hearing that word from him—"stop"—would make me better. It didn't. My skin still burns. I am not all better. In fact, it had no benefit. I wish I could blame someone or something for this.

I didn't e-mail Dr. Richard much after I got that e-mail from him saying the correspondence was inappropriate and should stop. For a long time, I forgot about the Myspace account. I figured it was dormant, but occasionally I updated it with my thoughts and feelings, then erased everything.

In the spring of 2007, I wrote the following Myspace blog post:

> *I can't sleep tonight. I keep thinking about the way it would feel to be with Dr. Richard. I imagine him touching me. I take the medication every day, but my thoughts are not going away. I want him. Jack has been awful ever since it happened. He is cold as ice, and the worst part is that I'm trapped, because I need the health benefits. I need the medication. He won't work through the issue with me. He forbade me to discuss it. I can't talk about it with anyone, because it is too much for polite conversation. I feel trapped inside myself. The memory of Dr. Richard's touch is all I want to think about. All I want to remember.*

I felt devastated that the physician had asked me to stop writing him. His rejection of my love further wounded my already-broken self-esteem. The purity of emotion I first felt at the thought of him ached inside my heart. My secret became toxic. Every time I used thoughts of Dr. Richard, I saddened. Sometimes I waffled in my thinking. I searched for the thread of reality that made my experience make sense; other times, I accepted my fate and blamed my illness for everything I had experienced. I learned to ask people questions when I was unsure of my surroundings. I checked in with my family and health care team often. What I learned was that real things happened but I misunderstood their meaning.

Dark Days

After my hospitalization, I began to recognize the difference between my beliefs and the events happening outside me. I realized that license plates appeared in random order, recognized that music on the radio was not written with me in mind, and accepted that road signs weren't cryptic messages to me. However, once I began to experience reality more concretely, it pained me to remember my thoughts. Every time I became conscious of how much I had misinterpreted Dr. Richard's behavior toward me, I was reminded again of how unloved I felt. I tightened my muscles and curled my toes against the floor when anything triggered memories of my psychosis. It upset me at my core level.

I still noticed secret messages—from music on the radio, creepy personalized car tags, and missing socks in the dryer to the color red, NO TURN ON RED traffic signs, stray black gloves, the smell of urine, and messages in my inbox—but I also knew now that I actively sought them out, that they were random events with no hidden meaning.

I tried to move on. I pretended like it had never actually happened, because I couldn't talk about what bothered me—it was a socially unacceptable conversation topic. So I ignored everything bothersome or strange. I was afraid to blow my cover by acting out in any way, and in time I learned to fake a calm composure when unsure of my surroundings, or to ask questions of the people around me. I trusted others were not psychotic or delusional and took my cues from them. My internal state was largely invisible, except to the very observant.

I especially wanted to trust Jack, but after everything that had happened, he never treated me the same. He disdained me. I tried, but things changed between us irrevocably. I needed his employee health benefits, because there was no Obamacare yet. I didn't have a full-time professional job. Now that I was supposedly well again, getting a divorce no longer felt like an option any more than getting a nanny had.

Every week I went to visit Harrison, and every two weeks I saw Dr. Bouley. After some weeks, the frequency of the appointments lessened as I stabilized on my medication and began my journey to healing. My medication check-ins lasted only about twenty minutes; the only things Dr. Bouley ever asked me about were my symptoms. When I asked him for my diagnosis, he said, "Postpartum delusional disorder."

During that time, I also started to write about my childhood. I needed to understand myself and why I got sick the way I did. Struggling to deal with the factual reality that my brain chemistry had malfunctioned and the signs I saw were my own imagination creatively interpreting reality, I desperately searched for a narrative I could accept. The further away from the perversion of psychosis I got, the more I realized my belief in God was important, because it made me feel safe in an uncertain world. And the more I wrote, the better I could reflect on what had happened to me. Part of me wanted to keep living in the memory of an alternate reality, though. It stung my soul to come back.

In early 2007, I got a call from Dr. Mitchel, a manager at a local insurance company. We had met a few days before at a New Hampshire Health Coalition meeting, and I had impressed him with my ability to organize data and analyze information to create a report on the cost of nontraumatic emergency department encounters in New Hampshire.

Dr. Mitchel had read my report about the lack of access to care in New Hampshire and asked me to interview for a part-time job. I enjoyed writing reports, and I had many friends in public health from my volunteer work experience in the community, so I agreed.

I spent between twenty-one and twenty-eight hours per week

teaching and working as a faculty member on a grant project. I drove my blue Subaru station wagon all over New Hampshire, training physicians to screen preventable illnesses in babies and toddlers. Jamie had started at a Montessori school in the fall of 2006, but I still volunteered at her child-care co-op.

When the laundry piled up on the dresser in our bedroom and Jamie's toys littered the living area, the tension over chores mounted between Jack and me. He stopped making eye contact with me and was short with his replies. On a Saturday in the spring of 2007, Jack and I sat down on the sofa in the living room. We had come to a divide that morning over the state of the household. He didn't understand why the house wasn't always neat, and he wanted me to work harder.

Sitting together, we counted the money in our brokerage, planned for college savings, peeked at our retirement account, and played with planning calculators. We had many conversations while facing our respective laptops; we were happiest when we were together in front of Microsoft Money and Quicken, because it was something we both did well. We'd play around with ideas of how to spend our estimated budget surpluses from Jack's bonus of $7,500. I was responsible with the budget. Jack usually was, too.

"Let's make a list," Jack said. Inspired by the computer game The Sims—where the characters have a happiness meter over their head—we listed all the chores in our house that had to be done. We each rated how much we liked or disliked doing each item on a scale of one to five, one being the most tolerable and five being the worst. Then we assessed the time each chore took and assigned specific tasks to either Jack or me.

It turned out folding laundry was the least pleasurable chore (it rated a five on the scale), and that was self-evident based on the piles of laundry inside our house. At the end of the conversation, we agreed on one thing: there was more work than either of us wanted to do—a total of 12.5 hours per week of housework and chores. We had already hired a cleaning company to clean our home. There wasn't much left to outsource. Somebody still had to pick up dry cleaning, sort mail, pay bills, and so on.

"Since I work full-time, I get forty hours' credit. You work only part-time, and you don't make what I make," Jack reminded me. He typed into the spreadsheet and gave himself 100 percent full-time equivalency but gave me only 75 percent for my value. He said he was being generous. Jack based my value on the corporate work I did, dismissing child care and volunteer work outside the home, whereas he had taken all these management training courses and thus saw himself as having more value outside the home.

I wanted to work through things together, so, rather than walk away from the table, I caved and agreed to his 75 percent assessment of my contributions.

When we talked about the spreadsheet with other people, nobody could understand Jack's logic. "Why is Sunny worth only three-quarters of a person?" everyone asked. People found it funny that we approached our relationship with spreadsheets in hand, but how else could I account for my differences with Jack? He clearly didn't think we were equal partners. Working, mothering, trying to escape my psychological triggers—my mind was slowly recovering, but it wasn't enough for him.

Meanwhile, I was still using Dr. Richard's Myspace account to write blog posts regularly. They were my only way to say what I felt. Two and a half years into my illness, by December 2007, I had started to realize the long-term impact of Dr. Richard's touch and the way it changed my life, and I posted something that must have shut him down: *Your touch is electric. It is like nothing I've ever felt before. Why didn't you go home to your wife that cold and snowy morning? You should have gone home.*

The fact that he chose to stay that morning, rather than go home, changed my life. While I would have gotten sick anyway, I probably wouldn't have gotten sick for him the way I did.

The Myspace password changed shortly after that. And I was locked out.

A week later, the doorbell rang. I had just gotten home with Jamie.

When I opened the door, a certified letter was wedged in the screen door. There was a green card to sign and send back in the mail.

I wondered why the edge was sliced open, as if cut by a razor. I pulled out the letter through the opening and felt unsteady and light-headed. Blood pounded in my ears. I could feel bile climb up the back of my throat as I saw it was a legal document, and addressed to me. I walked into the living room with Jamie on my hip. I sat down on the sofa with her and started to read silently. When she squirmed, I let her down, but she cried—she knew something was wrong.

"Uppy," she begged, pulling against my pants.

I ignored her as I read the letter, palms sweating, breathing shallow. I felt waves of emotion pass over me while I skimmed the pages. It was from the Roundtable Associates retained by Dr. Richard in connection with my postings on the Internet. They asked me to remove any websites and other online content. They reminded me that I had told Dr. Richard I experienced delusions, and that they would have no choice but to pursue legal action if I didn't comply.

Overwhelmed by a feeling of rejection, I sat down and shut down. I couldn't connect to my baby as she cried for attention. I couldn't think; I could barely breathe. I sobbed uncontrollably, with my face buried in my arm on the back of the sofa. Then, as I recovered my senses, I did what I needed to do. I gave Jamie a snack, unloaded the groceries, and started dinner. I felt numb. I was in shock.

When Jack got home that night, I showed him the letter and told him what I'd done. He told me to remove all content from the Internet and not to reply to Dr. Richard. "Not another word about this," he said.

I went to my computer and deleted the accounts I'd created in response to being locked out. I felt painfully alone in my dysfunction. Jack hated my problem, I wasn't allowed to talk about it online, and my only refuge was my journal.

Early in 2008, a few weeks after I got the letter from the law firm, Dr. Mitchel told me we needed to talk privately. He had just come back into the office from a big meeting. I was working on a project for the health program in my office when he burst in. He hung on to the doorknob and waited for me to look up.

"Tell me what happened with Myspace. I heard from the chair of the health coalition that there's a problem with something you posted there." He sat down across from me and looked at me over my desk. "I'm sorry to have to ask you this, but did you sue a physician?" Dr. Mitchel asked with a look of bewilderment.

"No," I said, disoriented by the questions.

"Well, there is a rumor spreading around the health coalition, and I need to understand what happened," Dr. Mitchel said.

"Well, I did have postpartum depression and told my physician about that, and he did refer me for a psychiatric exam, but I didn't sue anyone." Then I smiled halfheartedly, trying to reassure him, but I was distracted by the clock: it was already 5:00 p.m., and Jamie's school was very strict about on-time pickups.

"You need to go, don't you?" Dr. Mitchel asked.

"Yes, I'm sorry. My daughter's school closes soon," I said. He left my office with a concerned face, and my anxiety and post-traumatic stress shot through the roof. I thought I might barf as sudden, intense paranoia overtook me. What had happened? Who knew? What had been said?

When I got home, I called my social worker. When Harrison called back, I told him what happened. He suggested I stick to the argument that it was a rumor.

"What about the letter from the lawyer?" I asked.

"Just say it was a rumor," Harrison advised.

When Jack got home, I told him what had happened at work. He sat down with me. "You never should have posted that on the Internet," he said. "You may lose your job over this. The only thing you can do is tell the truth. You have to sanitize what happened and be honest."

I thought about it nonstop until I went to work the next day. Once I settled in and got coffee, Dr. Mitchel came into my office.

"I'm afraid I have to have you come with me to talk with Tanya in HR," he said. Tanya was the head of the human resources department.

I put down my coffee and stood up slowly. I could feel the blood rushing to my head and pounding in my ears. Horrified, I focused on taking one step at a time. I followed Dr. Mitchel down the hall, past the reception desk, up the stairs, to HR.

We didn't talk until we reached Tanya's office.

"I'm sorry we have to ask, but as the professional relations department, we need to know what happened. We were told by a very well-respected member of the coalition that it is inappropriate for you to serve as a representative," Dr. Mitchel said.

I felt devastated to hear the words coming from his mouth.

"Tell us what happened," Tanya said.

"I had postpartum depression, and there was an exam during the labor where my physician, the one you mentioned, touched me intimately. It left me traumatized. I was so sick," I said, as my tears began to fall.

"So I started a Myspace account and a blog and blogged about what happened. Then I got a letter from Dr. Richard's lawyer asking me to remove the blogs. I did. There was never any legal action. I never sued Dr. Richard," I said.

Tanya handed me a box of tissues. Dr. Mitchel shifted in his seat.

"What would the CEO say if he knew the whole story?" Tanya asked.

"He would say it's a terrible story," I said, as the tears flowed down my cheeks.

After a few seconds passed, they sat with me as I struggled to regain composure.

"I'm afraid we will have to take this to him," Tanya said. "Why don't you go back to your desk, and we'll let you know after we meet with the CEO?"

After I stopped crying, I walked down to my desk. I trembled as I sat in front of the computer, trying not to cry again. My future depended on the way this man responded to the rumor.

My coffee was cold by the time Dr. Mitchel came down. "It's okay," he said. "The CEO said he'd support you in whatever you want to do. If you want to continue as the company representative for the health coalition, then that's fine. If you do not want to be part of the health coalition, that's fine, too. Just know that you have the support of the company in this."

I choked back my tears. The company was treating me like a human being.

I kept working. Once Jack finished dinner and Jamie was in bed, I was alone. I'd sit in front of my laptop and spend time in our hot tub, out under the stars. I started writing more than journal entries. I began to write about my life and my story. There was nobody to talk to on those cold and lonely nights. Jack had installed a net nanny software that allowed me to visit only a few websites. I figured out how to skirt my way around it, but for the most part it deterred my lonely, desperate desire to connect with others to share my experience.

By early 2009, things were going better for me again. I continued to work, mother, and volunteer. Communication with Jack was still difficult. On a cold evening, in the midst of a terrible economic recession, Jack joined me in the hot tub and told me he'd heard a rumor that there were layoffs coming at the investment company he worked for.

"You're still the smartest person I know. But just in case you are laid off, we have the savings, and I can keep working. We could always sell the house and move in with family, too," I said.

"Actually, I don't think that will work," he said.

"Why?" I asked.

"I already called my mom. I lost my job today," he said.

I swam over and gave Jack a big hug, and we both broke down and cried. We cried out of fear and uncertainty. We hadn't suffered a loss like this since Jack's dad had died. As the breadwinner, Jack provided the health benefits for our family. I needed expensive medications and my first thought was, *How will we make it?*

"I'll call human resources and set up a meeting to discuss health insurance options," I said. The insurance company had increased my hours to the point that I qualified for benefits.

For the next three months Jack surfed the web by day, and we ate a lot of peanut butter and jelly. We tightened our budget and spent less money. It was a challenging time. When I got up to go to one of my three jobs, I'd get angry if Jack slept in. It made things tense.

Even with three jobs, I didn't make enough money to cover the mortgage payment, but at least we had health insurance through my work. Then, in March, a few jobs in the New York City area opened up, and Jack applied. My brother, Erik, lived in Park Slope, in Brooklyn; I immediately called and asked if he would put Jack up on his sofa for a few nights so he could interview. There had been a few jobs in the Massachusetts area, but nothing interesting. The two jobs in New York were dynamic: one in finance, the other in entertainment.

After a few trips to New York to interview, Jack landed a new job. We were excited and terrified when he got the offer. It meant we'd have to relocate. We sat down, and at first we assumed we'd have to move to the suburbs. Then we started talking.

"Where are we going to live?" I asked.

"Don't most people live in New Jersey?" Jack said.

"But we won't know anyone in the suburbs. How will we meet people? I'd like to live where we know people."

"Erik's wife said Park Slope has the best schools in the New York City public school system," Jack said.

"But Erik's condo is so expensive—what is rent like?" I asked.

"I will look into it, but I agree. Let's trust Erik and Cara's judgment," he said.

"It will be nice to live near family again," I said, and Jack nodded.

Jack went down for two days in April to look for a place for us to live, and he found a three-bedroom apartment in the heart of the South Slope. The nice, sunny unit was the best choice given the options we had. Jack moved to Brooklyn two weeks after he got his job offer, and I stayed behind in New Hampshire to fulfill my work contract. In my spare time, I mapped out the new apartment to determine what furniture to move and what to get rid of.

I had spent all my free time trying to fill this giant home in New Hampshire with objects that I was now giving away, all the while asking myself, *Why? Why did I feel compelled to fill my home? What madness inspired me to behave this way? How did I become such a consumer?* I reflected, as I loaded up the back of my station wagon with goods to take to the Salvation Army, that the last seven years of my life had been filled with pointlessness.

Jamie and I lived together alone during the week and drove down to New York City every weekend to see Jack. We'd go to Prospect Park and spend time with Erik. Between the rent, the mortgage in New Hampshire, and everything else, we had little money to spend. Everything in New York seemed so expensive. I refused even to buy curtains for our apartment. Jack bought them. It was too hard to think of giving away what I'd spent seven years collecting to move.

When I finally did move to Brooklyn, in July, the insurance company agreed to let me coordinate their program from New York. I worked about ten hours per week and spent the remainder of the time managing the culture shock of moving to Brooklyn.

The most traumatic part was having an independent four-year-old, who had no concept of an intersection or traffic, on the streets of Park Slope. Growing up in rural New Hampshire, Jamie didn't see sidewalks in our neighborhood; there was more forest than pavement. The differences between the city and the country overwhelmed me that first summer in 2009. My anxiety walking with Jamie, holding her hand, was palpable. The sedatives I was still using helped take the edge off, but occasionally I'd catch people taking photos of me on the train. I felt paranoid and tense; when I talked to my sister about it, she figured I looked out of place in my New England wardrobe of capri pants and sweater sets.

"They probably thought you looked like a tourist," Chloe said.

In time I adjusted, though, and the sounds and sights of the city became less jarring. I stopped being so tense on the subway. I learned to stay seated until the train stopped. I learned to anticipate the two-second delay before the subway doors opened.

On the home front, however, things with Jack continued to be as tense as ever. He didn't like the way I dressed or how much weight I'd gained since I'd been hospitalized, and he refused to see my strengths. He saw only my flaws, and he made a point of telling me about them. He'd say cruel, just barely audible things in a nasty tone.

"Excuse me? What did you say?" I asked him one day, after I thought I heard him say, "You're such a fatass" under his breath.

"You must be deaf, too," he said clearly.

"No, really, I didn't hear what you said," I said.

He glared silently at me, refusing to answer me.

Over time, those looks wore on my self-esteem, and I continued to struggle to feel confident walking along the New York City streets. I figured Jack's job was stressful and he didn't know how to cope with it, other than to play computer games and act mean. I didn't see the face he showed strangers on the street, but people sometimes looked at Jamie and me with concern as we walked along and Jack walked two paces ahead—so fast that I would overheat from my medication. When I'd ask him to slow down, he'd simply say, "Can't you keep up?"

One night this happened as we passed an older couple strolling along Ninth Street, past the music club Barbès. Jack and I had a date that night, and I don't know why he was in such a hurry to get home—we had child care, Jamie was fine.

The woman pulled on her partner's arm as they watched us pass. When I scurried by, I heard their chatter.

"That behavior of his is unforgivable. It's the type of thing that is subtle enough to go unchecked but over time takes a toll," the woman said.

"I hope she gets away from his emotional abuse," the man said.

When I heard the man label Jack's behavior as emotional abuse, I was ashamed of myself. I couldn't believe I'd let myself sink into this situation. I'd read Gloria Steinem and Virginia Woolf. I loved stories with strong heroines and had worn the title "feminist" with pride as a young woman. But after everything I'd been through, I needed the medication and health benefits. What choice did I have to get out? I didn't even have a full-time job. We'd promised "in sickness and in health," and we'd meant it, but this was not the future I'd envisioned when we married. Listening to strangers' observations created a more accurate assessment of my reality. Those people were right on: I was emotionally suffering, but I refused to acknowledge it. I didn't think I had choices anymore.

NYU

Cold rain blew against the windows, and gusts of wind howled against the glass. Heat from our cast-iron steam radiators made the apartment cozy. It was a typical Saturday night in December: Jack played video games in the front room he'd set up as an office space, and Jamie slept in her bed. The light bounced off the decorative plaster molding from above where I sat on the sofa. I had checked all my work e-mail and made a list of things to do for the start of the new week. Working ten hours per week was not enough; I had too much free time. I spent about three hours every week just parking the car, and I still stockpiled like I lived in the country. Every week I'd plan out the menu and shop as if there were no stores around besides the Fairway market in Red Hook. Jamie was in a Montessori program in Park Slope, and I walked her each way to and from school.

Sitting in front of the green Dell laptop, I shopped for Christmas gifts to ship out to Kansas City for the holidays. Between purchases, I decided to type into the Google search engine my dream job: research, New York City. To my surprise, a link to a research group out of New York University showed up in my query as the first link. I followed the advertisement. That evening, I started composing a cover letter to submit with my curriculum vitae.

I got the job. It took several weeks to process the paperwork and put me into a group of new hires for orientation with the human resources department. They scheduled my first day in February 2010. The week before the new job started, I decided that Jamie needed after-school child care. My commute into Manhattan from Park

Slope would take forty-five minutes under the best circumstances, and I didn't know whether, as a new employee, I would be able to leave early to pick up Jamie.

I posted an ad on Craigslist for an after-school babysitter and received many replies. When I read the response from Ava, a nursing student, she seemed like a good fit. She commuted from Staten Island to downtown Brooklyn for her nursing studies and called to schedule a Sunday appointment to meet with Jack, Jamie, and me.

Earlier that Sunday, I hosted a parenting workshop in my living room. Ava arrived as the last parents left. She was Puerto Rican, with long, curly, dark hair and big brown eyes, and knew how to connect with people. I felt an instant attachment to her and loved the way she interacted with Jamie. Knowing that students were required to pass background checks for hospital rotations, I asked to see Ava's driver's license and nursing student ID. I felt nervous about my first day at NYU and trusting Ava to care for Jamie, but I didn't need to be—Ava would help with everything.

Now that I had more free time, I decided I needed to do something fun for me that spring of 2010. Jack had started taking scuba lessons after he bought a Rolex; he felt like an impostor without a hobby to explain his $7,500 watch. I used my budget surplus to sign up for a Gotham Writers' Workshop course: Creative Writing 101.

The third night of class, the teacher gave us a writing assignment. "Write about something that happened recently that you remember made you feel something," she said.

I thought back to that morning. I'd had a meeting with my boss, and after the meeting, we had waited in the hallway for an elevator. I knew there were people in the organization I had yet to meet, but I didn't know it would be only a matter of time before I'd know them.

"Dan." Dr. Cullen called down the paneled hallway toward a fifty-year-old man in a dark sport jacket, who turned at the sound of his name as he jammed his ID badge back into the holder around his neck. He looked distracted when he stared straight at my chest. Then his eyes slid down to my hips, doing an equation, as if he were calculating my breast-waist-hip ratio. When his eyes landed back at my breasts, he studied me intensely, and I felt as if he were counting my breaths.

The way he looked at me made me feel desired. I clenched my toes in my black pumps and dug my nails into my palms as I held still, letting his eyes roam over me. I forced myself not to cross my arms as my breathing intensified.

"Dan," Dr. Cullen kept repeating. Finally, Dr. Cullen's startled voice raised the researcher's awareness. Dan paused and held still before he slowly lifted his gaze to mine.

I held my chin up and met this man with my steady observation. I felt desire flood my senses. The way this man made me feel—*I want to feel like this again.* He smiled slyly at my blatant desire, until he saw me begin to blink back my thoughts.

I'm not like he thinks. If he knew what I've been through, he could never want me. I wish it had never happened. I closed myself to the idea of him. He didn't understand. I blinked back tears. He looked at me hard, shook his head, and stared intently as I struggled to maintain composure.

I thought back to the comment Jack had made about my pink cardigan and trim pencil skirt as I'd left the house that day. "You're wearing *that* to work?" he'd barked, minutes before I needed to take Jamie to school.

"Yes," I'd said, and Jack had merely glared at me. I'd felt terrible all day about the way I looked—until the researcher looked at me and made me feel things I'd forgotten I knew how to feel. I'd been deprived of desire for too long.

That evening in my writing class, I wrote a story about meeting the researcher. After I described our first encounter in the hallway, I recorded my reflections on various events: *I wish it had never happened. The way Jack treats me isn't fair. It has been five years; if I were just stronger, I would leave, but I'm not strong enough. I need another year before I'll be ready.*

The blank pages filled up with my handwriting. I started to think again about the possibility of one day breaking free from Jack and making it without him. I'd come a long way since my days of not being able to imagine coordinating child care—now I had regular help and a full-time job with benefits. The steady work flow was the best medicine I'd ever taken.

One day, Dr. Cullen came over to my desk and said he needed a favor.

"I need a sticky note with just the word 'why' on it," he said.

I was in the middle of projects, so the memory was vague—in fact, later I would sometimes think I'd made it up to explain what happened next. A few weeks later, I flipped through the notebook and found one of my sticky notes on the page. It was in my handwriting, but I didn't remember having put it there. The note said, "Why?"

Was it the note I'd made for Dr. Cullen? Was someone messing with my notebook? I flushed. I never responded to that note, but I became somewhat paranoid that someone might be checking my desk. Even though it was my note, I knew I had written it about something else. How had it ended up adhered to that entry marking the page?

I put the notebook in the back of the drawer and threw out the sticky note. I knew I should just act as if I didn't think anyone had a clue about my secrets and deny everything.

One night every week, I had my writing class. I'd bring a small canvas tote for a notebook, textbook, and homework to go in—my writing bag. One day, I got to class and went to pull out my notebook, but it was a new notebook. My coworker Tina had given me only one notebook like the one in the bag, so I was surprised to discover a crisp notebook in its place. I didn't think about it too much; I just let it go. But it started me down the path of having multiple notebooks for class assignments, instead of a single notebook, and that annoyed me.

I also found that my pens went missing. I started to develop a strange affinity for pens, because I could never find a pen when I needed one. That fall, I returned to teaching part-time, in addition to my research job. I'd store my handbag in my desk at the research center, because I had not been assigned a locker. One night when I got to the front door of my brownstone apartment building, I couldn't find my keys. Ava was home with Jamie, so she buzzed me up. I used the guest set the next day. When I got to work, my keys were lying on my desk.

"Thank God!" I said.

"Did you forget your keys?" Tina asked, as she saw me staring at the keys next to the keyboard.

"I worked late teaching last night. I must have dropped them on my way out," I said.

"You're lucky you found them," she said, sharing a story about a family member who had been robbed recently. Tina sat directly behind me, and sometimes I overheard her talking on the phone. Then, if it got serious, she'd hang up, go to Dr. Cullen's office, and shut the door to use his office phone.

That left me near the front door to open it every time someone came to the door. Every employee besides Tina and me lost their ID badge at some point during the grant application process. Someone always needed to be let in.

As time passed, I learned that Tina kept keys hidden for Dan. He knew where she kept them, and some days he hid them in hard-to-find places. She explained that the researcher had a nightly habit of stopping by the office to sign papers for her. It was their game.

One morning, I noticed Tina tearing her desk apart. "Tina, what's going on over there?" I asked.

"I know my keys are around here somewhere," Tina said. "Where did he put them?" she asked herself.

"Who?" I asked.

Slowly, Tina turned toward me to answer. "Dan," she said, looking up at me as I stood by the file cabinet with my coffee, making my social rounds, trying to connect with coworkers. It was a quiet office space—too quiet for me at times.

"Why would he move your keys?" I asked.

Tina laughed.

Dan and Dr. Cullen were well known for their humor. On conference calls with other research groups, the NYU team leaders made the best jokes and had more fun than the other groups. After this happened a few times with the keys, I decided he knew Tina well enough to know that it wouldn't severely unsettle her to have her keys go missing, but would fluster her just enough to take her edge off.

Around the holidays, I forgot to take my medication for two days. The third night, as Jamie, Jack, and I sat in our dining room for a family meal, I said, "Jack, I just realized I forgot to take my medication for two days." I leaped up to get the pills from my bottles, stashed in a decorative wooden box with a gray elephant painted on a red background.

"You shouldn't take that stuff anymore," he said.

I paused. "You think I can stop?" I asked.

"You've been fine for years. I don't think you need it anymore. It was probably just hormones from the pregnancy," he said. "You made it through the move without symptoms. You have a full-time job at NYU. Why do you need to keep taking the medication?"

"I think I should keep seeing the psychiatrist. I'll call him and let him know I fell off the meds. I'm just not comfortable stopping without consulting him," I said, sitting back down to dinner obediently.

Over the next few months, in the spring of 2011, I worked on an application for a $100 million grant, and I posted anonymously on a psychology website about how I felt.

My only concern now that I've stopped the medication is when I feel attracted to anyone other than my husband. I worry and obsess over the idea of developing erotomania. The psychiatrist thinks I feel guilty, and he suggested something that sounded like a Freudian theory and started asking about my sexual-health history prior to my mishandling by the physician at my daughter's birth. He was pondering whether there was some other trauma. If only it were so simple.

Wouldn't it be nice if psychotic mental illness were something you could talk yourself out of? I tried to explain to him that I lost the battle with logic the last time I lost touch with reality. I'm just not sure that someone who has always been sane can comprehend the experience of psychosis. My delusional beliefs were so emotionally connected that for me they didn't easily respond to logic. I think I am an intelligent person, and I tried very hard to overcome the delusions, but there is this emotional response that is so intense. How can you turn off the emotions for an alternate reality? I doubt many people could overcome psychotic mental illness with logic alone, and I think we know very little about our own emotions. Emotional health and well-being is mysterious. I don't think we really understand the science behind it, either. He could tell me only that there is a rule of thirds: one-third of the people get better, one-third get worse, and one-third stay the same.

I was worried I'd develop symptoms that would put me in the "get worse" group.

My attraction to Dan had taken on a life of its own. I didn't want to fall for someone I couldn't have again. I worried on the Internet psychology forum that my delusional condition, erotomania, would return, only this time Dan would be the object of my desire.

Reluctantly, I agreed to work over the weekend to help with the process of the grant application just before it was due. During this intense time, as I worked to meet the deadline for the three-hundred-page document, which laid the framework for a way forward toward comparative-effectiveness research in health care, my bond with Dan deepened, and I found my close contact with him to be more and more intense.

In the meantime, I felt less bonded with Jack. We were having sex only once a week at this point. One night, just when we were starting to get into our missionary-style sex, the bed began to slide against the hardwood floors; then we heard a loud *pop* and saw smoke and a flash of light. Jack and I were both startled, and the bed felt electric. Plus, we were a little drunk. It was a Friday the thirteenth—May 13, 2011. He had me smell all the outlets, but I didn't detect any smoky odor coming from them. We had lost our arousal, and Jack decided against doing it again. He went back to finish his computer game, and I fell quickly asleep that night.

Monday morning I went in to work and saw a penny lying on my desk. It was tails up—a sign of bad luck. I wondered who had left it for me. Did they know about the lamp? The same week the tails-up pennies started, I found out Jamie's kindergarten teacher would be let go, and I read in the *New York Times* that our local firehouse would be closed.

I refused to acknowledge how much these signs bothered me, but every time a new one came, I inventoried my desk, going through everything and cleaning, dusting, and straightening up. I felt like my neighborhood was being played with. Was the tails-up penny a sign about the events unfolding in the local government around my neighborhood, or, scarier, was it about the accident with the bedside lamp? Thankfully, these symbols of bad luck didn't happen every day; they came in fits and spurts.

A few days later, we were getting ready for work, when Jamie came running into our room and jumped on the bed. We saw a flash of light and some smoke, and heard a *pop*, and this time we didn't let it go. Jack cleared us out of the room and searched. He found the lamp cord compressed beneath the bed frame, with the copper wire exposed on both sides in two places on the wire. The circle crossed the cord in two patches. It looked like a black-and-copper equal sign.

When I got to work that morning, I found a second tails-up penny. Then I got a phone call from Jack's mother, who said she needed to talk with me.

"What is it?" I asked.

"I've been wrestling with this for a few weeks, but when I was with Jamie a few weekends ago, she said her daddy hurts her. I need to tell you and ask you if you think it's true."

Although hearing her say that upset me, I also knew what she was referring to. "I know what happened," I said, as I excused myself from the small research space to take a walk. "Jack tossed Jamie into bed one night when she didn't want to go to sleep." The intensity of his anger was related to the challenge of parenting. Every day I woke up and treated our relationship as a blank slate, but his aggressive behavior took a toll over time. "He is so angry, he doesn't know his own strength," I said. "I don't think he meant to hurt her." But as the words came out of my mouth, I knew something needed to change. I needed to protect my daughter from her father's behavior.

I wrote about my response to the tails-up penny in my work journal. I left the papers there overnight, then shredded everything the next morning. At first I wrote about how I wanted Dan, and my erotic fantasies about him. Then I shared that things with Jack were becoming increasingly difficult. I could not be near him without suffering his poor treatment of me, and when he started directing his frustration at Jamie, I felt isolated and uncertain.

At work, I saw words in the search history on my browser— "passwords," "yahoo," and "nyu"—that I didn't remember having typed into the search engine on the laptop. Considering the fire and the subtle demand for passwords scared me. I'd seen the sign in the drawer with the hanging file tab that stated "computers." I'd been getting subtle messages in my environment for a while. The hanging file tab with the word "computers" happened at work after Jack had told me he'd read of black bag jobs where corporate security specialists go in at night and copy everything from employees' computers. I figured someone was sneaking into my desk at NYU and leaving me hints about their snooping activities. I knew better than to write anything about how I was feeling in e-mail; somehow a digital footprint didn't feel safe after seeing the "hanging" file tab with the word "computers." I imagined I'd hang for my writing what I was feeling and leaving traces of my experience digitally at work. I recorded the passwords to my Yahoo!, NYU, and Amazon accounts in one of my spiral notebooks that I kept in my desk. The drawer was crowded with notebooks. After what had happened with the lamp cord, I didn't know what to do. I wrote pitiful, desperate notes desiring the researcher side by side with notes about my fear of Jack and whoever was getting into my desk and putting my life at risk with the lamp.

On my Kindle app, a book on attachment parenting appeared. I downloaded a lot of parenting books, but I'd never heard of this one, *Beyond Consequences, Logic, and Control: A Love-Based Approach to Helping Attachment-Challenged Children with Severe Behaviors,*

Volume 1. I had recently been approved for an Amazon credit card and gotten a $50 sign-up bonus, which had apparently paid for the book, but I checked the account history and couldn't remember having either signed up for the credit card or ordered this book.

My iPhone was also acting very strange. When I opened e-books on it, I found them open to certain passages, as if they were giving me specific parenting instructions. I knew I was never a perfect mother, but I loved Jamie more than anything and I wanted what was best for her. When my iPhone started playing this game with book passages, I played back.

I opened Lisa Kleypas's book *Where Dreams Begin* and highlighted a passage that read: "You'll never be as vulnerable as you are right now, and therefore any decision you make should not be trusted." I chose that passage because I related to the character on a deep level. I didn't believe that I could trust my decisions in my situation.

When I went back into my Kindle app next, I saw the cover page of the sequel to the first parenting book, *Beyond Consequences, Logic, and Control: A Love-Based Approach to Helping Attachment-Challenged Children with Severe Behaviors, Volume 2.* I thought it was giving me biofeedback, but it was too special to me to share with my friends and family. Later, I'd reflect that I should have taken the phone to the Genius Bar at Apple and asked for a complete reinstall, and should have involved HR sooner, but at the time I was afraid. I just hoped the person sending me these messages was someone who loved me.

I decided to write about what was happening. I explained the experience with the hope that one day I'd understand. I knew for a fact I had become sick, because nobody I trusted could believe my stories, but technology triggered me. However, in spite of my constant fear, I was able to function in even the most delusional states. I got up, took care of Jamie, and went to work. I wrote papers and did my job. Granted, I worked with a great team, and a solid group of researchers with whom I verified my work. I knew how to cope. But too many things didn't add up.

One thing I was worried about was that Jack might retaliate and destroy my work. I wanted to hide it somewhere safe, and the only place I could think of was under my desk. So I filled a large blue shopping bag with all my journals and took my manuscripts to NYU in May 2011.

When I settled in at work, I checked my search history and again saw keywords that I couldn't remember typing: "trust," "debonding," "letter," and "distance." It reminded me of the way I had felt when I'd gotten those wrong-number calls all those years before. Was I just paranoid, or was this real? I felt the wave of emotion flood my senses at the thought of being loved. Was it Dan? Or—my heart skipped a beat—Dr. Richard? I knew it was wrong that I wanted to believe in my unrequited love. Everyone still tried to tell me Dr. Richard didn't love me, but I didn't want to believe it. I couldn't stop loving my memory of his touch.

Then I flipped through my work notebook and saw the word "coercion" underlined. I didn't remember having underlined it; was I being coerced into action? I'd written that I had worried about my anniversary dinner and that I didn't want to be with Jack ever again. Concerned that there might actually be someone coercing me, since I couldn't figure out the lamp situation, I wrote a letter saying I trusted whoever would help me get away from Jack, but I didn't really know whom I trusted.

Hacked

I saw the bolded text in the browser, and my computer was behaving strangely; still, people I trusted told me I was just sick, that it was impossible that anyone would hack me. But nobody looked at what the computer did. I was never able to replicate its actions and show the computer to an independent observer, but it was so real to me in the moment.

On the night before my tenth wedding anniversary, I sat on the sofa. The memory stick was in the computer, and I was backing up documents to the cloud, when I saw my C: drive disappear. Taking its place was a single foreign drive on my Dell. I didn't know what it mapped to, so I clicked on it to explore. It was filled with files of my work, organized strangely. How had someone found all my e-mails and saved them as .txt files? I didn't know how to do that. I went back a level to search for the rest of the files on my laptop. There were no files on the computer. I panicked and took out the memory stick. The drive disappeared, and my files returned. Fascinated, I put the memory stick back into the computer. I didn't remember having saved these messages. I suspected someone had tampered with my flash drive when I opened my coffee-table drawer and found a fancy pocketknife inside.

The file organization started with projects I had done over the years in grad school: reports, papers, and research summaries. As I clicked through each item, I was impressed. It looked like a portfolio of everything I had ever worked on and spent time to create. I enjoyed looking into my files like that. My favorite rediscovery was the science fair project that Jamie had worked on to measure and record her

entire stuffed-animal collection. Then came the pictures. I started to
tear up as I saw beautiful moments of motherhood flash before my
eyes—pictures I'd taken of Jamie playing at the park, pictures of her
all dressed up and happy, smiling for me, her mom. Then I got upset
when I saw pictures of Jack leering at the camera. I remembered how
angry he had been at me while I'd taken the photo. It ripped at my
core. Why did he look at me that way? It inspired me to decide that
I needed to finally get out of the situation in which I felt so helpless
and trapped.

Reading people's affirmative e-mails to me and seeing professors'
comments on my graduate coursework liberated me from Jack's
degrading view by reminding me of the quality of my work and the
beauty of my personhood. Professors' feedback, colleagues' letters
of reference, and friends' words of love and support piled up on the
mysterious drive, and I cried as I read them.

Then the browser launched a few different websites. A comic book
that popped up on a health-promotion website reminded me of my
story with Dr. Richard, in that it was similar to my birthgasm. The
web page described the adventure as a two-team, good-versus-evil
event. I became transfixed by the idea in the story. I skimmed over
Dr. Richard's battles and studied my own. I saw the graphics tell me
I'd get sick again, then fall in love with a foreign man. They showed
me trying new things I didn't know I'd liked, and then there was this
picture of what looked like a swirling cauldron. In the graphic, the
man and I looked down at a dark pool. We stood near the edge, where
a plank went out over the water. It made me think of the fiery pit in
The Lord of the Rings, but maybe it was just a diving board over a
pool. The man I loved explained the financial meltdown; then he was
carried away to prison. Then I lost my vision. The comic book ended
with me looking back at the story.

During my tour of the Internet that weekend, as I started seeing
bold text on the browser telling me all these things, I decided I must
be insane. I figured, to be on the safe side, I should go back on my
meds. I walked over to my wooden box with an elephant painted on
it, opened a bottle of antipsychotic medication called Abilify, and
took a full dose. When I checked my browser history again, I found

"why take pills" in the toolbar search box. Then I asked how the browser knew about the pills, and I found bold text highlighting the word "listening" on the next page I visited.

I turned on some music for whoever was communicating with me, not really believing that it was possible to be experiencing what I was experiencing. I couldn't believe someone would choose to target me and play with me so intensely just to be nice. But so far, they seemed nice enough. When I asked "where are you?" in the search, a picture of a map near JFK airport appeared.

I thought about calling my psychiatrist, but he wasn't available on the weekends. I decided I would make an appointment first thing Monday morning to tell him what was going on. I couldn't believe I was so sick. I was delusional, right? It hadn't happened like this before. I had never had such crystal-clear communication and imaginative experiences. Who would ever believe me? If I told people about this, they'd think I was full of crap. So I decided I'd document everything for myself and keep writing instead. That was all I could do. But when I read the bold text in the browser, it triggered me to start looking for signs all around me again. I didn't know where this invisible person's power to interact with me ended.

The next page that opened was that of the Central Ohio Fiction Writers' Ignite the Flame contest, announcing that they had extended their deadline. I went back to the mysterious drive, opened a story I'd written that Dan had inspired, and submitted it to the contest.

Excerpt from the Ignite the Flame contest submission "Winter Storm"

She lifted her hand to her hair that had come undone from her bun at some point during the evening and swung it to one side of her shoulder. Her breasts were still standing erect as if they hadn't been informed that her orgasm was over. She simply looked at them in delight. "I've never seen my nipples look like this before."

"It is a very becoming look on you." He winked at her.

She blushed, which he thought strange after all they'd shared, another tribute to her recent loss of innocence.

"You must let me see you again." He brought her hand to his mouth and kissed her knuckles.

"Thank you, but you cannot. For I am afraid I would be ruined." She looked like a woman having second thoughts. "My guardian didn't arrange for travel when he sent for me."

"Guardian. You didn't warn me. Am I going to have some old fellow hunting me down asking me to come up to scratch?" Daniel asked.

"Oh my lord, had the thought occurred to me I should have said something, but to be honest, I don't think he thinks much of me. Since he took me on, he hasn't ever sent for me before, even the holidays were spent with the staff at school. In fact, we have yet to meet."

Unease crept over Daniel as he thought of his ward traveling from her school over the next week sometime. But surely she wouldn't have received his request so soon. If this was his ward, he was the world's greatest cad.

He leaned his head back against the pillow before asking, "Do you know who I am?" When she didn't answer, he lifted himself up on the elbow and looked at her deeply. "Have you any idea, because I am beginning to think I know who you are," he said.

A few weeks later, I got an e-mail from the contest committee. I'd lost. In fact, my entry had placed dead last in the competition; I had received the lowest marks of all the works submitted. They told me the hero was a cad and the heroine was unconvincingly innocent. I was disappointed. It was depressing to see how poorly my work had been received. I didn't understand why the browser had told me to enter my story in the contest. Did it want me to realize that I was writing bad romance? I figured if it could communicate with me, either there was someone doing this in real time and I had choices, or time was predetermined for us.

One morning during this time, I walked toward the subway after dropping Jamie off at kindergarten. I had an appointment with a lawyer in Manhattan to try to plan a way out of my marriage, but by the time I reached the Bank of America ATM in Park Slope, just before the subway stop, I was too afraid of what the *New York Times* app on my iPhone was telling me to get on the train. The material I'd read was so alive and vivid to me. I'd just finished a story about inequality, when I stepped over a pile of about 150 Equal artificial sweetener packets, spilled on the sidewalk on Tenth Street. The packets spoke to me in a deep way. Then, when I passed my building, I saw that someone had left books on the stoop. One book was a story of a woman finding herself in Tuscany after a divorce; another was on meditation and healing. I thought someone was giving me clues that I needed a divorce and some meditative healing.

Then the messages intensified as I began reading a story about the British royal family. The text got to me. It was as if someone were walking along next to me, telling me what I was feeling in response to feeling played with. They knew how it felt to be hacked. I stepped into a bank doorway around the corner from my home, and tears streamed down my cheeks.

It wasn't my spam talking to me this time; now the *New York Times* app was observing my response to the situation and telling me how it thought I was feeling as I walked along the streets of Park Slope. It told me I would be afraid. Was somebody watching me? I was in the grips of intense paranoia.

I tried to find the phone number for my psychiatrist, but my hands were trembling too badly. I could barely manage. When I saw my brother's phone number, I aimed for it with my shaky index finger. It took two attempts to land right on his number. Erik had been at a friend's beach-house share over the weekend and was in a crowded car, on his way back to work in the city, when I called.

"I need your help," I choked out, terrified to be saying it aloud in public.

"What? I can't hear you," he said. "Hey, guys, quiet down. It's my sister—something is wrong."

"I'm scared," I said, my voice quivering as I stood in the doorway, facing the corner. "Can you come help me get to my doctor? I can't find the number, and I need help."

"Yes, just give me half an hour. We're almost back. What's wrong?" he asked. "Is everything okay with Jamie?"

"Jamie's at school, she's okay, but I feel sick," I said, as waves of emotion threatened to overtake me.

"Are you gonna be okay till I get there?" he asked.

I choked out, "Please come soon."

"Where are you?" he asked.

"I'm at the ATM by my house on Seventh Ave.," I said.

"Go get a coffee, and I'll be right there. It'll be okay. I'm here for you," he said. After I hung up, I walked to the Connecticut Muffin, where Erik had said his friends could drop him off, in the heart of Park Slope. I reopened the *New York Times* app and started reading again. My hands visibly shook, and tears were streaming down my face. One woman saw me crying, did an about-face, and walked the other way. Her nonverbal communication—that act of turning her back on me—made me feel painfully isolated, rejected, and stigmatized. Her brief eye contact showed that she was afraid of my tears, when what I needed to feel in that vulnerable moment was the calm of love and acceptance.

I opened my writing app, called My Writing Spot. I needed to record what was happening with my phone and my experience; I knew nobody would ever believe the *New York Times* app could have been hacked by someone trying to speak to me. There was one bolded line in an article that particularly captured my attention. I studied the text: "Leader of Egyptian Islamic Jihad." Then I read it backward, and new meanings presented themselves. Did this mean that if God had instant messages, Jesus wouldn't have died for our sins? I sounded out "Die." Then JC meant Jesus Christ. And when I read IM, I read Instant Messages. A represented America, L stood for love, and I translated "sina" to "sinner." Was it why General Electric was for a deal?

Messages were coming at me rapidly in my wildly stimulated state; words and signs kept blossoming into new strands of thought. The only way to gain control over my thinking was to define terminology that I could live with. I created a code set to interpret the English language based on delusional love. While I waited for Erik, my medication still hadn't taken full effect, so instead I created a safe space within my psychosis by using semantics and the code for love. As afraid as I felt sitting on that bench, I fought back against my fear by identifying concepts that held deeper meaning for me than the messages I was seeing in bold print. I typed into my writing app a list of what letters in the words meant to me. I used the alphabet to define words that I could live with. I focused on protective concepts. A few of the first definitions I created were:

> A = America
> C = see
> D = delusional
> E = energy
> L = love
> M = mother, God, love
> O = orgasm
> S = Sunny, science (rare)
> T = the physician
> Y = why

My new language had a very limited vocabulary, using only the definitions I wanted to see. I was into it because it always sent good messages. As I sat with my iced coffee, I calmed down, knowing I was safe within the personal meaning I assigned to the messages in the *New York Times* articles I was reading.

Another mother sat down across from me with her child and looked at me curiously as I waited for Erik at the Connecticut Muffin. Her calm acceptance of my crisis further reassured me. This woman, unlike the last one, wasn't afraid of my tears and public display of emotion.

By the time Erik arrived, I had finished my coffee and my tears were almost dry. The thought of God instant-messaging the world to save Jesus had lifted my spirits, and I filled the pages of my digital log with my thumb, typing about what was happening to me.

As I started to explain to Erik what was going on with the *New York Times* getting hacked, he quickly helped guide me back to the apartment, where we could talk in confidence. I told him part of the story. I even told him about the comic book on the health-promotion website. I told him that the comic book told the story of my birth-gasm with the physician, then showed me getting sick, Dr. Richard making deals in dark rooms, and me falling in love with a man. I didn't tell him that in the comic book I was wearing a collar and being led around on a leash, looking down over a swirling cauldron, before my lover was taken to jail. Or that the physician would turn angry for a while.

Mostly I told Erik that I was afraid of Jack. I was afraid that he would be so angry at my rejection of our marriage that he would hurt Jamie and me, and that I needed to get Jack out of the house. He was not a violent person, but he was so angry with me and our life, I needed out from him. I was so afraid to try to make it on my own, I couldn't escape my fear. Yet at the same time I felt coerced into action.

I believed that Jamie's and my ability to continue living depended on getting away from Jack, but I couldn't figure out a way to explain to my family the way I perceived the threat with the lamp as the tip-ping point. I'd told them about the lamp, but I was too afraid to tell them what it meant to me. I mean, what if the threat were real? And, I didn't want them to doubt my motivation, because emotionally things were over with Jack.

I told Erik I was sick again but that the lawyer had said Jack couldn't call my mental health into question as grounds for child custody. I was afraid I'd lose Jamie, because Jack always told me that was how it would happen. But the attorney had assured me I would not lose my daughter.

When I went to search for the website of the lawyer I had origi-nally consulted, the Park Slope Parents' website listed only one lawyer: Green Resolutions. What had happened to the name of the other lawyer? With the *New York Times* speaking to me in new ways, I felt even more paranoid.

In my state of fear after Jack's mom had called to say he was hurting Jamie, I'd e-mailed my family to share what was going on. I'd explained my fear of Jack and my experiences since Jamie was born, journal entries and all. In sharing my story, I finally felt heard. It was a beautiful feeling to connect with my family over my story, to be embraced by their love and warmth, and to narrate my experience the way I wanted to explain it, including the birthgasm and my psychosis. In some ways, writing about what happened let me reconcile my identity after I'd been sick. All that helped me to finally feel whole again.

Everyone e-mailed back about the story with notes of love and support, and commended me for having completed a first draft of my story. Most read the first draft within a day or two of getting the e-mail, although my dad had my stepmother read it first when he saw the chapter title "Birthgasm" in the table of contents. My stepmom, Jill, edited out the portions that would make him uncomfortable and summed it up for him after reading it. "Some things a dad just shouldn't read, but I love you and think it's great that you're writing about it," he told me afterward.

My sister called me up when she got the e-mail. "Wow, this must have taken some time," she joked about the length of the attachment, which was hundreds of pages. "I went to print it and ran out of ink," she said.

When I talked to my mom, she said that I needed to hire an editor to carefully copyedit the work. But she'd also never known what I'd gone through before, so she cried a little when we talked. "I didn't know that's what happened," she said.

Erik hadn't read it. "You told me the story, and I'm here with you," he said when I asked him what he thought. "I'll read it after it's published." He said all this to me while we were sitting in my psychiatrist's office, waiting for him to show us in. During that appointment, the doctor told me to continue taking a full dose of Abilify. Erik told Jack he needed to move into a hotel, because he was no longer welcome in the apartment.

When I got home, I broke out in hives and started vomiting from the stress of having asked Erik to kick Jack out. Ava was there to watch Jamie after school. I kept throwing up, and Erik went to get a change of clothes and his Dopp kit to stay over.

I was so confused about whether or not things were really happening. There were so many things going on at once, but I knew one thing wouldn't change: I needed Jack out of my life, and after I'd met with the attorney, I knew there was a way forward. I didn't have to keep living with his cruel emotional treatment of me; this wasn't the dark ages. When I'd looked at the research on the outcomes for women who left abusive relationships, I'd read that they were often no better off than they would be if they stayed in the relationship without emotional support. But I knew hope was real. Treatments that were relatively safe and effective were available to me, and I was able to work.

The minute Erik called my mom to explain what was going on with my illness and with Jack, she booked a ticket to New York. Erik stayed on the couch and helped until she arrived on the next flight from Kansas City. The medication sedated me, and between that and my physical reaction to the separation, I was struggling. Jamie went to school every day, and I took the week off from work to adjust to being back on the medication. It was so confusing getting sick at the exact moment I extracted Jack from my life, because it affected me physically, emotionally, and spiritually. But I realized I'd be sick for the rest of my life if I stayed with Jack.

My thoughts about my crush on Dan made me feel desperate and pathetic. I knew it was impossible to feel this way again. It lasted for a few days, until music in iTunes broke my heart. The iTunes Genius feature made me think some secret agency was in control of the music I listened to. The songs iTunes suggested were amazing love songs. They fed my delusional love until "Father Figure" by George Michael played. My feelings turned off when I heard him. I couldn't feel things for Dan as I listened to that song, because the words made me think of my father and reminded me that Dan was too old for me—I was young enough to be his daughter.

The moment when my feelings shifted was when my computer

launched iTunes and began playing a *Weeds* episode in which a drug kingpin, U-turn, is laid to rest in his hot tub. The actors explain that U-turn wants to be buried with his boat, but they can't fit it in the funeral home. When the video opened automatically on my laptop, it confirmed that I was not to love the researcher, because the character was dead on the show. The clip of the funeral played three times before my computer let me return to my browser. When that happened, Dan's spell over me was suddenly broken and I reverted to loving Dr. Richard.

I laughed and sobbed simultaneously as I watched the show and my heart broke free from Dan. Coming back to reality was a painful emotional journey, but the humor in my strange experience made it hard to take things too seriously. I didn't like to change perspectives. It was always easier to stay in one reality than to visit another. The transition stung my soul. Knowing that I was broken and that neither Dan nor Dr. Richard welcomed the intense feelings I experienced created an invisible force of energy that sucked me in. It was impossible to feel desire for Dan or the physician while knowing it wasn't wanted and that I was on my own to cope with these feelings. But that wasn't the only problem with this condition; I also had to fight constantly to gain control of my mind.

But I couldn't control the way I experienced reality when I was being played with like this. It was too much. The hacked online content I read was still triggering me to search for signs everywhere, and the bold text that kept appearing told me I was being taught lessons. The "first lesson" my browser taught me was a news story about a Southern mayor who was doing something foolish, imposing a short-term solution to an extremely long-term problem with the utilities in his city. I didn't understand why my browser took me there, but I retweeted the story. In fact, I documented my response to the entire hacking on Twitter when the browser would let me. Social media helped me cope with being hacked.

The second lesson my browser took me to was an audiobook on ethics. The main theme of the lesson was that all world religions are based on a simple concept: "do not use or accept force." In other words, don't make somebody do something, and don't let somebody push you around. I thought it was ironic, considering how I felt coerced. It was wrong for them to lead me around, and wrong for me to follow.

The browsers began fighting with one another for control over my Dell. I sat on the sofa, watching the browser wars, and couldn't figure it out. I rebooted, and while I waited for my computer to restart, I searched my iPhone and found a video in which Steve Jobs spoke about Apple's role in the international information age, and about China specifically. I figured the Chinese were in competition with whoever had hacked my system, but there was so much activity in my browser, I couldn't determine a single force influencing me anymore.

Back on my phone's mobile Twitter feed, I was directed to a link that allowed me to watch part of an anonymous group's video claiming that the money for the US financial bailout was being diverted to foreign investors. The group wanted to see the 1 percent suffer. The video disconnected just before the ending.

I also reflected on a book I was required to read for my master's program, *The Dance of Legislation* by Eric Redman. The book is a tale of how policy happens in Washington—a mysterious story about how power is used and laws are made, sort of like the Netflix series *House of Cards*. When I asked Google what happened to Eric Redman, I discovered he lived in Texas and was dealing with oil. I asked why they would put him in a dirty business like that. They responded, "Trust," in bold text. I concluded the oil industry was one where they needed to trust someone. I responded by googling people I'd known in Boston's financial district who mentored me while I cared for them as their health care provider. I searched for information about the men my instincts told me to trust.

My reading agenda during the time I lived in Boston was influenced by one man in particular, Robert. During the tech-bubble crash, he reassured me, "These things are not new. Markets have survived these types of things before. There is a really well-done book about it. You and my wife are both gardeners, and she liked it, so I think you'll enjoy it, too." He told me to go to the public library's main branch and check out the book. He wrote the name down on a piece of paper for me. I checked out the copy of *Tulipomania* that was housed at the library. When I went a few years later to recommend the book to someone else, the version sold by Amazon was not the edition I knew. I must have read an older, rarer edition. My version was a beautiful book with a three-inch-thick spine and colorful plates of flower prints throughout. The book described the history of tulipomania, and the Dutch tulip-market crash. Robert was Dutch, too.

When I typed Robert's name into the window and touched the search button, the browser took me directly to a report by an oil company where Robert sat on the board. The browser shared information about the corporation's activities near Cuba. I trusted and cared for Robert, but I had no idea what to make of that, and something about the browser launching, independent of my keystrokes, and directing me to documents that seemed questionable, bothered me. After all, I had no idea who controlled my browser. The worst idea was that it was a group of trolls from one of the websites Jack liked to spend time on.

My experience of getting hacked occurred around the time the Stop Online Piracy Act (SOPA) legislation almost passed. SOPA gave media companies property rights over all the personal content on individuals' computers if they were found to possess any unlicensed content.

The last destination the hackers took me to was a website where I could download music. I had never illegally downloaded a song before that night, but the browser wouldn't release me from the site without my choosing a song. I finally selected one, called "All Too Much." The bolded text that emerged in response said, "Nobody ever selects that." I chose that title because I knew I loved all too much, and I wanted to feel loved all too much in return, too. But SOPA laws would mean that the corporations would own all the content on my computer because I'd downloaded that song.

The hackers eventually dumped my browser at a survey center. I quit the session and listened to iTunes. I wished I hadn't been so taken by feeling special because of my experience. I wished I'd trusted Jack, an information security professional, but I didn't. I chose the oddly behaving computer, with the memory stick inserted, and hope for my belief in love, over my broken relationship with my husband. I wanted the information being presented in my browser to be real. Being led around the Internet fascinated me. Seeing the information about me on my C: drive made me feel loved.

I struggled to know the line between my reality, which people shared with me, and my perception. When I went online, there was no way to be sure I saw what others saw. I felt isolated artificially and susceptible to manipulations.

I decided it couldn't be real—it didn't pass the Occam's razor test: the principle of parsimony that states the simplest explanation is usually the correct one. This was not simple. I wished there was someone I trusted who could help me, someone with the privilege and power of knowledge. I needed to be patient. Trust takes time. I felt foolish for thinking I was being cyber-stalked. People told me that I was just sick. It was the easiest explanation. The only choice I had was to think it was my sickness and try to document and test it when I felt able.

I had read that Dr. Richard served as a member of a political group. There were lots of people who could benefit from harming him with a story of his back-and-forth technique during my orgasmic labor. I thought back to the phone calls that started me down the path to losing my mind in 2005–2006 and came up with several possibilities.

It was all random. This was the only option the people who loved me wanted to believe.

Someone was watching me and chose to harass me to the point that I would feel triggered and would break.

Republicans or Democrats were destroying young, promising politicians.

The physician loved me, and his method of revealing his emotions was flawed. I worried I created a web of confusion. I'd sent a message to a man I'd met online and shared a photo. I'd bcc'd the message with the image to Dr. Richard. The more I thought about who could be involved, the more confused I felt. I wished I hadn't bcc'd that message and pornographic picture to Dr. Richard back in 2005.

Researchers were looking to undermine my group, like those in competition for the $100 million grant.

Time travelers? Delusional, right?

Someone was sabotaging me.

Industrial espionage?

Organized health care? Health advocates might want to sabotage me personally for their political gain.

When I thought I was being led around by the Internet, I did what the bolded text required. I changed my Facebook page. I thought I was the first person allowed to post a music video on Facebook. Then I got a spoofed e-mail, where the name when I read it backward told me to tell all, but when I opened the e-mail it came from someone with a different last name than in my inbox. The spoofed e-mail from an e-book publisher spooked me.

A week after my delusions led me back to loving Dr. Richard, Erik hosted a party on his roof deck in Greenpoint. He had separated from Cara, and he was enjoying his bachelor lifestyle. I arrived early, and we sat together for a while and talked until I started to nod off. He needed to start getting ready and left me alone to prepare for guests. Every time I opened my browser, I felt like I was communicating with someone. I felt isolated amid this new experience that I was navigating my way through, and by this point I'd tapped out my closest friends and relatives, but I still needed to feel supported. The browser took me to a live chat room where two people were logged in. I heard a chipper female's tone and a thoughtful, masculine character. They were discussing what a person needs to be resilient. But by the time Erik had finished his chores and had come out to check on me, the conversation had vanished; there were no messages bolded in the browser, and no chat room to show Erik when I tried to explain what I was experiencing. I didn't know what to do, and Erik didn't understand what I was talking about. When he checked the browser history, it was blank. I worried him. So I stopped trying to make him understand.

Once friends started to arrive and I was able to connect with people, I felt a second wave of energy. Many of the members of the party were former Kansans. They listened to me when I told stories. "I was talking with my dad earlier this week, and he told me some interesting stories about the founding fathers of Cair Paravel being mistaken for a division of the Posse Comatatius."

"Uh, what is the Posse Comatatius?" someone asked.

"An underground militia located in the continental United States whose movement Dad said was documented in the local papers back in the eighties. He said one of the dads was a Green Beret who wore his field gear on a field trip to my dad's land with the kids. The dad went to use a pay phone in a small-town grocery store. It must have spooked people, because National Guard helicopters arrived while the dads cooked dinner. Everyone was surprised by the commotion. They had to explain who they were to the National Guard, and why they were training kindergarteners to survive in the wild."

Our friends laughed at the thought of my sister, Chloe, on that trip as the founding fathers tried to teach her to survive in the wild at age five.

"What were they thinking?" someone else asked.

"Probably Armageddon," Erik said.

"They learned what not to do based on the reactions from the oldest children, like Chloe," I said. "She still freaks out about having to pair up with a partner to prepare the chickens for dinner on that trip."

"I'm glad I'm the youngest," Erik said.

When everyone kept asking me if I'd tried someone's grandma's cookies, I felt paranoid. I worried about those cookies. Were they laced with something? The last thing I needed was drugs to screw with my chemistry. I'd shared more than I knew I should about my story, but it was nice to bond with friends. My mom was watching Jamie at my apartment, so I decided to leave around ten. When I got home, Jamie was fast asleep.

It was tough going back to work after my week off. When I got to my office, I started to cry. I wished I wasn't at work. Had what I thought happened actually happened? I stared down at the handwritten "Winter Storm" story sitting on the top of the pile of notebooks in my drawer. My back was to Tina; I didn't want her to see me in my emotional turmoil. When I had first gotten in, I had told her that Jack and I had separated, and I'd explained that I'd broken out in hives and had the stomach flu or something the week before. She gave me space and didn't ask too many questions.

After I cried, I hid in the bathroom for a while. I imagined I was in nature, out in a canoe with the dragonflies. I sat for so long on the toilet seat that my legs went numb. I could feel the imprints from the toilet seat on my thighs when I finally got up. I wondered why the seat was so high off the ground. I was not a small woman, but the seat made me feel like a child. Then I remembered it had been the men's room before they'd renovated. Before I left work, I filled my blue bag with the journals I'd brought to my office for safekeeping. When I got home, I unpacked the contents and noticed immediately that things were not as I'd left them. My red notebook should have been on top, but it was missing. Instead, the journals from my hospitalization were there, bookmarked on specific pages.

Why had the red notebook disappeared? When had the work notebooks disappeared? Would they be returned? Who had taken them? I was afraid to say anything about it—I did not dare bring attention to my potential paranoia—but I did mention my problem to my brother. He worried about me when I told him these things. He assumed I'd lost touch with reality, and was mistaken, but I looked everywhere for the entry recording my first impression of Dan. I wanted to read it again; plus, there was some useful work information in my notes. I also talked to an old friend from high school, who said she thought the cleaning crew at work was messing with me. She told me stories she'd heard from friends who worked on cleaning crews, but Francis and Joey, at NYU, were good custodians.

When my mom and I returned from shopping one night that week, we saw a harvest sunset over the Gowanus Canal as we looked down Ninth Street toward Red Hook. I'd never seen the sun look so large along the New York City horizon. My mom gave me a worried glance when I pulled out my camera to take a photo; then she turned to face a small, vibrant green van parked in front of the fire hydrant. It was painted with a giant bird of paradise advertising spiritual healing. My Twitter account feed had buzzed all day with doomsday prophecies about the end of the world being near. I felt safe in the knowledge that a van with spiritual healers was near, should something go wrong for me. Mom looked curiously at the van, shaking slightly, but I was calm. I trusted things would be okay. But I didn't take another picture, because I didn't want to seem paranoid.

When my mom and I got home, we sat at the kitchen table, talking about how I would manage life after Jack. The radio was playing in the background. I usually listened to 103.5 FM, I Heart Radio, in New York City.

Suddenly, a sexy man's voice interrupted the music to say, "Sunny."

I looked at my mom and knew she'd heard it too. "You heard it, right, Mom?" I asked.

She nodded, slightly shaken. "It's just the radio, though. It sounded like it was part of the song," she said.

Late in the night I slept on the sofa, with my computer by my side. I watched the hard-drive light flashing against the darkness. In time I saw the flashes like codes blinking to me, and I listened to the music that played on iTunes when "100% Pure Love" played. I heard the word "blade" in the song.

I lay back and felt myself enter a game.

In response to the call to arms of the word "blade," I quoted Shakespeare. "The pen is mightier than the sword."

Then I found myself wondering if I was passing though a maze game in the ancient Mayan tradition. As the Mayans predicted the end of modern time to occur that year, 2012, I found myself up late that night. I considered who could be leading my browser. Jack had the most access to my computer, so I would have suspected him of hacking me, but he offered to check my computer out when I complained early on about it. I even fended him away from the computer when he became suspicious, saying I'd reboot to deal with the glitch in behavior on my own. I didn't let him help me, because the strange files on the mysterious drive captivated my attention. I wanted to know more. My curiosity led me to trust the mysterious drive over Jack. It didn't make sense that it would be Jack, he didn't want to separate, didn't want change, and was reluctant to move out. Erik had to have a talk with him to get him to move out. Plus, he had rules about personal privacy. I couldn't imagine Jack violating me that way. It would have been against his ethics to hack me. Even if he wasn't loving me, he knew right from wrong in a digital environment. My instincts told me Jack wasn't to blame, because he'd never appreciated me or my work that way.

I knew I was sick, but things still happened that I couldn't explain. Things went missing. I saw signs. I hated seeing them. It made me feel sick. Sometimes I pretended that I didn't notice, like a photo that I'd posted on Facebook after an ancient Native American symbol alerted me to a sign. When I took the photo, a sword appeared in the image. I posted it on Facebook, and one of my friends saw the grim reaper in the photo as well. I had not touched the photo to edit a thing. The picture of the sword and the grim reaper were in the Con Edison building window on Flatbush Avenue in Brooklyn. It was just a defect in the glass's antiglare material, I told myself—except I saw a prehistoric symbol of the sun cross, a circle with a cross in the center.

When I thought too hard about all the signs and messages, I worried. I tried not to think about how the lamp cord got under the bed, sparking and blowing smoke and fire when Jamie jumped on the bed. But it concerned me enough that I decided to write a letter to my city councilman, as a way to document the incident in case something serious was going on. I got paranoid and deleted the original letter. In the re: section of the letter, I said I was a fire-safety activist. I shared the story about the lamp catching on fire, interrupting our sex. Even though we lived a block away from the firehouse and I felt safe because of that, I made sure that the city councilman knew I was probably not the only person in Park Slope at risk of this type of event. Death by fire and sex would be a shameful way to go. The cord must have slipped under the bed, creating a potentially deadly situation.

I wondered if anyone read my letter. If they did, I never heard about it. And at work, I decided to keep quiet. If my notebooks landed in the wrong hands, I would be screwed. But why would anyone be in my desk?

I continued to have theories about all these connections for the next four to six weeks as I wrestled with ideas about everything that had occurred in the short span in which I had seen my computer act up, separated from Jack, and become ill.

"On"

In mid-June 2011, I donated to the Obama campaign and signed up to volunteer. The browser took me to strange art photos and a psychological-profile assessment. I picked the photo of the food, rather than the lonely man standing alienated and alone. I had no idea who was gathering the data I shared, but it was a few weeks after the initial hacking. I got an e-mail that I was "in," and I signed up for a fund-raising event in New York City.

They gave me a seat by the aisle in the back of the theater. An older woman with a cane needed a seat where she could extend her leg. I had returned the second ticket because Erik couldn't make it. So I went to *Sister Act*, the musical, alone. At intermission there was a slight scene when a member of the campaign staff tried to eject the older woman from her seat and give the spot to a young man. The woman guarded me from the seat change.

The woman stared down the man and whispered in a low tone, "I know about you and all your schemin' tricks. You'll hear about this if you try to remove me from this seat." The campaign manager looked a little bit curious about the woman's response to him, and he backed down. He couldn't physically remove the woman without making a scene. The young man looked very uneasy. I was thankful for the older woman sitting in the seat I had encouraged her to take. When I told my brother the story, he got upset. He figured I was still sick. I wished I knew a way to convince him that the incident I'd witnessed had taken place in real life.

After Jack moved out, I joined a depression meet-up and got out every week. It was hard learning to be social and learning to be alone.

I'd been married or together with Jack for over thirteen years. He had always been by my side. Because that level of companionship had become normal to me, I didn't adjust well to the lonely part of my new life in separation. The hardest part was when Jamie visited her dad and it was just me alone. Being social was exciting, but for the first time in years I didn't have anyone to measure my interactions with others. Jack wasn't there to critique my behavior after social events.

By the end of the summer, I decided I needed to either move to a new apartment or get a roommate. I found Sophie, a college student, through Craigslist. Strangely, I found a heads-up penny on the sideboard in the front hallway with a letter from her student-loan company addressed to my home the day after she agreed to be roommates. It was creepy. When she stopped by, I showed her the mail.

"Oh my God, but I didn't even tell them I was moving," Sophie said in disbelief. "How do they do that?"

I shrugged. After all the "omens" I'd experienced, I felt triggered. I mean, I thought about the options—the banks were buying e-mail information from Yahoo!, some agency was harassing me, or maybe someone from the future was helping me—but, unsure of the correct explanation, I gave up thinking about it and instead hoped the heads-up penny indicated that Sophie was the first sign of good luck I'd had in a long time.

Having Sophie around was good not just for me, but for Jamie, too. When I was too tired to do Jamie's two-hour kindergarten bedtime routine, Sophie would often sit with her to keep her company until she fell asleep. In September, Ava got her first nursing job and started working as an RN. When Ava couldn't pick up Jamie from school because of her work schedule, Sophie was able to do it. I reduced the amount of money she had to contribute to the household, and it helped provide additional stability for Jamie. Mostly it was nice to have someone home when Jamie was at her dad's part of the time.

When Jack came to pick up or drop off Jamie, he wouldn't make eye contact. He looked gaunt. He lost about thirty pounds within a month, and by the end of the summer, he looked like an entirely different person. After I kicked him out, he never connected with me again. He didn't even like to discuss Jamie. He'd just tell me his expectations and demands for our custody schedule. I'm not sure what I expected it would be like with him after I refused to continue our marriage. I would have thought he would be relieved, but his response was foreign to me. It was as if he didn't want to acknowledge what had happened.

Two months after Sophie had moved in, we had settled into a fairly normal domestic routine, but strange things were still happening, and these constant little reminders nudged at my well-being. When I cooked, I came to expect that the key seasoning I needed would be missing. It became normal to look for an ingredient that I had verified I owned before shopping but then couldn't find when I needed it. One day I'd have cinnamon, the next none. Then I'd buy more. I'd go to make vegetable chili, and the cumin would be missing. Then, a week later, making something else, I'd have three bottles of cumin. Dominated by the spice problem, my cooking suffered.

Work continued to be a stabilizing force for me. Despite my missing notebooks and the thought that someone was snooping about my desk, I found going to an office and writing kept me on track and allowed me to do what I loved and to stay connected to intelligent people who supported my academic success. But then, one day in October, I received a harassing phone call from a woman in NYU's administrative facilities department. She said Meirav Segal Weichman had asked for an ID badge from my department. "The man said he works with you. He said he works with Sunny Mera," she said.

"Who did he say he was?" I asked.

"He said his name was Meirav Segal Weichman," she replied. I scribbled down the name quickly.

On the walk to work, I always read graffiti for signs. When I read the single word "didn" in a piece of graffiti along the side of a newspaper dispenser, it bothered me that the "t" was missing and it didn't complete a thought. I sounded it out backward. Did it mean "need ID," or was it short for "die, Dean"? An overwhelming sense of fear filled me when I remembered seeing it.

"There is nobody by that name who works here, and Tina handles all that. Let me transfer you to her. Thanks," I said. I felt exhausted.

I transferred the phone to Tina, but she got cut off. When the call dropped, I told her, "I think you need to call the facilities department about someone trying to get an NYU ID badge. They're claiming they work with me." I started googling the names. I found a PDF listing the names of scientists, related mostly to physics and math.

I thought back to the story in the large red notebook, my secret, and I worried. Who was harassing me? Why would they say they needed an ID?

I saw my psychiatrist on Friday morning. I told him that I felt paranoid. When I asked him my diagnosis again, he said it was either "delusional disorder" or "intermittent psychosis." He agreed to increase my dose of Abilify to fifteen milligrams per day—five milligrams in the morning and ten milligrams at night—which should help when I missed and forgot doses. Also, it wouldn't sedate me as much.

Meanwhile, my burning skin was back. It had spread from my arms and shoulders to my stomach. I questioned why this had to happen when I was supposed to be in New Hampshire to speak at a meeting in just a week and a half. I knew my mind played tricks on me; I kept losing bits of memory, like when I had a button buttoned and the next time I looked down, a different button was buttoned, making me look unkempt. I fixed the button carefully. Then my hair clip moved from my pocket to my shoulder strap. I wanted to take a tranquilizer and go into a deep sedation, but I couldn't. I needed to stay focused and get through it.

A small white scrap of paper with a phone number appeared on the floor of the front hallway in my apartment. I googled the number. It belonged to an employee of Omnipoint, a telecommunications company. How had it gotten there? Was it tucked between the pages of the art history book that I'd looked up ancient symbolism in?

Then Sophie came in to chat, and on her way back to study, she took a minute in the bathroom to freshen up. When she returned to her computer, she screamed. Then she walked into the hallway that connected to the galley kitchen, holding a pink, size small girls' sock.

"Why is this on my computer?" she asked.

"I don't know," I said.

"What do you mean, you don't know? Why did you put a sock on my computer?" she asked. "Jamie, did you sneak in while we were talking? And place it on the computer?"

"No, I didn't." Jamie looked up earnestly with her apron on; she was helping me flip pancakes. "Mommy?" she questioned. But I knew I had been with Jamie the whole time, so I worried. But, not wanting to concern Sophie about the problem with things being moved about, I decided my only choice was to cover and lie.

"I must have dropped it," I said.

But I had been standing in the kitchen, making pancakes, the whole time. How had it happened? The only reasonable explanation I could think of—that I had time-traveled or been teleported—was impossible, right? Nobody in her right mind would consider that a reasonable explanation. It was not an option, I told myself.

I sulked to myself, hating that I had to be sick. The only way I felt safe was to believe I was sick, or that time travel and the good of humanity were real. Everyone I knew preferred to believe the former, so I sucked it up and offered a solution that Sophie and Jamie could live with.

That week, I fell off my meds. The stress of the harassing phone call and the confusion with the signs in our house contributed to a lack of organization on my part, and I missed three days of the medication. I went back on it as soon as I remembered, but I was struggling to remember to take it now that I was living independently.

It was a big week for me, too. I had a presentation in Washington, DC, at a research conference. I hoped I'd have fun with friends and colleagues. I felt closer to the military, so I felt safer. I had to have faith in humanity. Seconds after I wrote about feeling safer near the military in my paper diary, I got an e-mail: @MilitaryUpdates was now following me on Twitter. Then a defense contractor started to follow my Twitter feed, too.

I'll be okay as long as I can keep it together, I told myself.

At the conference, there was a filter on the lens of the projector. Everything the author intended to appear in red looked gray instead. My colleague who was scheduled to present before me stood before the group to give the first lecture in the session. The woman wore a bright red outfit. She tried to correct the color setting. The group of researchers decided there must be a filter on the screen because of the colors projected on the screen, versus the colors the author stated were on the monitor. The presenter was disappointed in the execution of her slides, because her red outfit intentionally matched her red slides.

Sitting in the audience, I joked with her. "Maybe this feature is why it's called the Lavender Room," I said, referring to the name posted on a plaque outside the door. "Everything intended to be red turns shades of gray."

The people near us laughed. The author gave up on the color deficit, and the meeting continued. When my turn came to present, I shared the slides. I was thankful that my trigger of my fear of God, through the color red, was muted to gray.

When I got back to my room, I checked my e-mail and read a story about the police killing people with mental illness in the NAMI New Hampshire newsletter. It spooked me so much that I was afraid to travel to New Hampshire for my presentation the following week.

When I opened my desk drawer at work the morning I returned from the Washington conference in the fall of 2011, one of the missing journals had returned. Under the journal, a stray adverse-event form was peeking out. It upset me that the notebook had reappeared. It was the journal entry containing the letter to my inner critic that my writing teacher had made me write to myself during my writers' workshop in summer 2010. The stray adverse-event form was turned to say "Possible Adverse Event" and the word "Date."

I sat and stared at the letter, stunned and unsure of what to do. I decided the form was a sign that I should probably try dating again. I didn't know what to want anymore. I had worked so hard for so many years not to act on my feelings for the physician that the thought of his sending me messages terrified me. I knew my love was inappropriate, but my undying hope that Dr. Richard loved me was my guiding star. It lit the way through the most terrifying times. But I decided maybe the sign was right. Maybe it *was* time to date. I was sick of being sad and crying myself to sleep every night over thoughts of what had happened to me.

I talked about it with my friends and family. Contrary to everyone's advice to keep my mental illness secret, I decided I wanted to be honest. As hard as it would be to disclose, it was the only way I felt like me. I needed to share in order to feel right about myself. My sister and brother thought I was intentionally trying to scare people away, but I just couldn't hide it. It was too much work and effort to pretend that I was "normal." Hiding it isolated me.

So when I talked to Chloe that week, she helped me to design my first online-dating profile. Within hours, my inbox had messages, but I was still focused on mentally preparing for my trip to New Hampshire. After I got off the phone with Chloe, I started packing for the trip. I set out suitcases and laid out clothing. While I was going over my checklist, I realized the GPS was missing. I knew the last place I'd left it was in the basement. I went to the basement and did not see it anywhere.

"Have you seen the GPS?" I asked Jamie when I got back up to the second floor of our apartment, where she was playing house, dressed in her Halloween cat costume.

"Nope," she said.

"Come help me find it," I said.

"Oh—I think it's in the bin in the kitchen." She joined me in looking in each bin, searching in the basement again, and looking through her toy boxes. Nothing.

So I printed out driving directions and found the car cell phone charger. We drove to New Hampshire relying on my memory. Jamie stayed in Boston for a sleepover at her grandma's. I left the conference early and drove straight home through Boston to pick up Jamie, then went on to western Massachusetts and Connecticut. There was no power at any of the rest stops along the way. Cars littered the sides of the road, abandoned and out of gasoline. A terrible storm had caused power outages all over the coast. By using common sense, I made it home safely on a single tank of gasoline with Jamie in the backseat.

A few weeks later, I was doing laundry in the basement. I found the bag with the GPS in plain sight by the storage space. How had I not seen it there? It was out in the open. I was sure I would have seen it if it had been there when I had searched for it.

When we got back into the city, I also checked the OkCupid application on my phone. There were several messages waiting for me. In the car service on the way home, I began reading them nervously. One was from a war correspondent from the *New York Times*. He was from Iraq. I began to wonder what he'd think of my birthgasm story. Was a story like mine capable of creating world peace? I wondered if orgasmic labor could redefine points of view on life and living. But the application froze and wouldn't allow me to reply to his message for a day. My mild paranoia suggested the idea of a dating branch at the CIA. I thought someone was manipulating my online-dating experience.

When my phone froze, I kept getting notifications that one of the OkCupid staff programmers was visiting my profile. I imagined the staff had noted my application was behaving strangely and was checking my account. I speculated the cause of the problem to be a group of social-networking advocate hackers sitting around, eating junk food and drinking coffee, trying to set me up with men by using their laptops and software packages to attack my computer and phone. In my mind the idea was bright, but I decided not to clear the idea with my sister, because I figured she wouldn't take my concern seriously.

My family did not believe the birthgasm story made me special the way I wanted to think I was, because they saw what had happened to me after the story of the birthgasm. When I broke from reality and was hospitalized, Chloe was the one whose phone I called in fear in the middle of the night, leaving messages that were confusing and painful for her to listen to. She had listened to all those psychotic ramblings, and she loved me anyway, but she refused to indulge my delusion that the birth made me special.

If I shared my thinking that my phone was hacked, I figured Chloe wouldn't even take the time to see what my phone was doing; she'd just want to talk me back to her reality, where I was merely delusional. I needed technical confirmation that I was paranoid, rather than rationalizing it away. I mean, I understood I was sick, but things happened.

When I finally restarted the phone, I was in the cab on the way home from dropping off the rental car at Avis in downtown Brooklyn. I shared a quick message with the *New York Times* reporter. We started to write. I shared stories about my missing pens at my desk at work. Eventually, we planned to meet. By our first date, we'd seen only a few pixelated photos of each other online. We located each other through text messages. He told me that he was running a few minutes late and instructed me to wait across from our Manhattan destination, Eataly, on a park bench.

The phone rang as I went to the bench and sat down.

When I answered it, I sensed he was on the prowl, and when I felt someone coming near me to sit on the bench, I intuitively knew it was he. I turned and smiled as I answered the phone, looking at him. He said hello, holding a flip phone. I heard the voice echo in my receiver. My intuition had foiled his plan. I asked him if he always tried to sneak up on his dates. He shrugged. He was taller than I was, and had dark hair, a handsome face, and a thoughtful presence. We had a pleasant evening, and when he said he thought I was beautiful as we sat at a rooftop restaurant, I started to get emotional. It took me a few seconds to regain composure. My mind played thoughts of the way things were with Jack, whom I'd separated from six months before but was still technically married to. I didn't believe his compliment as I considered what Jack would say.

On the second date, I invited him over for a cooking lesson. We made a soup with butternut squash in it. On our walk around the neighborhood after dinner, it was raining, and I told him that something had happened to me that I thought had the potential to change the world. I told him my hopes and dreams and explained how I thought the birthgasm and the idea of maternal satisfaction could change the world.

He explained the reality of the Middle East. A story like mine wasn't going to change anything. "Most people can barely read. It's another world there," he said. He shared how Western reporters twist news stories, writing what the West wants to read, and said reality is not as clear as the *New York Times* makes it out to be.

When we parted, he told me he felt lucky to have met me. I didn't know if it was me or if he had just had some really unpleasant first dates prior to me. I decided I should keep dating and figure it out. I kept working, mothering, and writing.

The following weekend, I was attending an association meeting in central New York, when the strangest thing happened. I sat alone in a large dining hall, talking on the phone with my dad. I stared at a chair, then turned away for the briefest of moments. When I turned back, three copies of NYU's *Nexus* magazine's "Access to Care" issue were sitting in the spot on the chair I had been studying before. Where had the magazines come from? I hadn't seen anybody drop them off. I turned away from the spot and turned back, and they were still there.

I started to sweat. "Do you believe in miracles?" I asked my dad.

"Well, yes," he replied.

I stared at the pile of *Nexus* issues. Had I been so focused on the phone that I'd missed seeing who'd delivered them? All I knew was that one minute the chair was empty, then I'd glanced away and they'd appeared on it. I posted the cover photo, of a ticket booth and a curtain, on Facebook, as documenting my paranoia on social media still seemed to be my most helpful coping method.

I started to imagine those three issues of the *Nexus* "Access to Care" issue to be a sign. After all, three was my lucky number. The issues had appeared on the chair in front of me while my dad had told me about his vision of becoming a missionary dentist who wanted to train dental therapists in Ethiopia. I didn't remember anyone's having dropped off the magazines.

I listened to my dad and looked over at the chair I'd been studying earlier, counting the axis of a square and the edges of the chair as I tapped my toes. Nobody believed in teletransportation. Somebody had put them there. But I thought I was alone in the room. I questioned how I'd missed the person placing the issues there. Had I dropped the memory?

The scheduled bus never came to take me and two of my friends home from the conference, so a Brooklyn bus filled with Seventh-Day Adventists offered to drive us back to New York City. The evangelical group sang songs and worshiped the whole ride. It was fun, but it made my friends uncomfortable. We made it home, and I settled in front of the computer.

After I met the reporter, on cold winter nights I started to search OkCupid, but I got very little response. That was how I met Garth online. I asked him for advice on what to do. He reviewed my messages and liked them. We became friends, and I started writing stories for him. As a former member of Romance Writers of America, I enjoyed writing about relationships, especially when I was getting to know someone. It was a way I could play with characters and increase intensity without feeling vulnerable emotionally.

Around the same time, I started messaging an Indian banker named Hugh. He had just returned from a trip to London. When I learned he was foreign, and because his name reminded me of the comic book I'd seen on the health-promotion website, I knew I wanted to learn more. He sent pictures of the estate where the conference was located. The breathtaking stone mansion was surrounded by grand gardens that sent me into a writing frenzy. I dabbled and played with our characters, sharing the real-life realities and financial uncertainty about the ending of the grant I was working on.

In mid-April, Jamie and I were back in Kansas City, visiting family, during her spring break. It was good to be there. While on a walk, I struggled with the idea of having to work in close proximity to Dan if NYU won the $100 million grant we'd applied for, because my attraction to him was still intense. I hated having to work with him, because it stirred my delusional thoughts and confused me. On that walk in Kansas City, I realized that I would never be satisfied by working closely with Dan. I would struggle whether we won the award or lost it. It was a losing situation for me either way.

While I was walking and worrying, my phone buzzed. It was Dr. Cullen, the director of the research team.

"We didn't get the grant," he said.

There wasn't much else to say. I needed to know, and I was glad he told me so quickly. I got off the phone and walked the rest of the way, unsure of what would happen next. I went to my computer and started to search. I applied for a few jobs and shared the news with my family. I cried some, drank some wine, and spent time connecting with Jamie.

After she went to bed, I spent the night writing romance and dreaming of finding someone who could love me. Garth wrote me back immediately, liking the new story, but I agreed to meet the banker the following week. Hugh was mysterious and different in ways I couldn't figure out. I wanted to understand him, and meeting was the best way to get to know him. I started writing him chapters of a historical romance novel as part of my seduction technique. I became increasingly intimate in sharing with him. I sent the first chapter of my book, the birthgasm scene, so he could understand better. He called me on the phone that same night. He wanted to meet. I agreed to meet him after work that week.

I nervously bumped his shoulder with my chin when we first connected. I felt a bit awkward under the blue arched ceiling at the modern lounge where we met. The drink menu was an education. Hugh ordered something with falernum in it, called Isle of Virtue—a name I found humorous and a bit pretentious for a drink. I played it safe and ordered something I knew: a gin and tonic with lime.

By the end of the night, we were next door at a tapas restaurant and Hugh was fork-feeding me bacon-wrapped figs stuffed with blue cheese and almonds. They melted in my mouth, and with his thick Indian accent he ordered the nicest bottle of wine I'd ever had. He said it was from a friend's estate in Spain. His friend owned the restaurant.

"There is something I have to tell you," I said, running my finger along the rim of the glass.

"Tell me," he said, facing me squarely from his barstool.

"Well, it's something that was the best and worst event of my life,"

I said. He looked at me curiously, with his dark gaze, and waited for me to continue. "It all goes back to the birth of my daughter. You know that story I sent you?" I paused and waited for him to nod. "Well, I had a birthgasm. It was one of those things that changed everything," I said.

"Tell me," he commanded.

I went on to explain all about how I'd practiced climaxing while pregnant and about how I'd begun fantasizing about Dr. Richard. He smiled back at me, asked for more details, then slowly sucked on a fried, salted bean.

"When the physician touched me, part of me was next to my husband, but the other part was in another world filled with intensely rich internal sexual stimuli. I lost myself in the thought of him and his touch," I said.

Hugh put his hands at my jaw and drew me to him. He kissed me with a passion that I surrendered to. I almost forgot we were in a crowded tapas bar in the Flatiron district after work on a Thursday night. I loved feeling the intensity of Hugh.

Hugh liked my story, and when he accepted me for having loved and lost, it felt okay. I also learned I wasn't the only one with a past. Hugh had made a name for himself during the US financial meltdown in 2009, when he'd been working in mortgages at one of the not-too-big-to-fail banks. The movie *Margin Call* had a character just like him in it. When I got home from the date, I knew I still needed to tell him about my mental health. It bothered me that I hadn't yet disclosed it. But I needed to.

In the meantime, I kept sending him my fantasies in the form of a book called *Lord Hugh's Desire*. As I sat writing, I couldn't stop remembering the prophetic comic book; I felt it was part of my prescribed destiny to at least try to know Hugh. When he invited me to the show *Venus in Furs*, I agreed. But before I would meet him again, I needed him to know my whole story. I sent him the memoir, including the scenes from the hospitalization. I cried when I pressed SEND, not knowing how he'd respond. But I'd rather know if it was a problem early, to prevent forming a bond with an unwilling character.

Late in the night, he wrote back, telling me he thought I was brave and that he looked forward to our trip to the theater that week.

I swiped my badge to get into the NYU research space on Second Avenue in Manhattan, where I'd been working for two years now. Our last funding cycle was ending that spring, and since we hadn't been awarded the $100 million grant we'd applied for, federal regulations mandated that the staff pack up the studies and put the research information into storage. That May morning, I sat down at my desk and thought back on recent events that had me unnerved. I read through my notes from the past two weeks.

It started when a pink IMPORTANT MESSAGE sign appeared on my desk on April 20. There was also a blinking light on my phone. I had a voice mail waiting. The woman whom I'd asked to call me back to confirm the delivery of instruments for a study had left a message: "I've called you, like, three times, and your cell phone just keeps ringing and ringing into space. So I figured I'd leave a message on your work phone."

I knew I had to take action when I saw the pink IMPORTANT MESSAGE pad. A year earlier, my coworker Meg had sat at my same workstation, and one day her own pink pad had gone missing right in front of her.

She freaked out. "Okay, who took my pink IMPORTANT MESSAGE pad?" she called out over the cube walls. "It was sitting right on my desk." She got up to walk around to each of us, looking at our desks.

I remembered it had been unusual for Meg to lose things; she was very organized and kept track of all the accounts. That weekend, I called AT&T. "I think something is wrong with my phone," I said to the technical support agent.

"Tell me what it's doing," he said.

"Every time someone tries to call me, they tell me the phone just keeps ringing and ringing and they never get my voice mail," I said.

"Okay, let me try calling you on another line. Just a second," he said.

After he'd run a few tests and checked the call logs, the agent determined my SIM card was bad. He told me I could get it replaced at the AT&T store in downtown Brooklyn. I trusted the sign that I needed to resolve the phone issue as soon as possible. Then I had software issues, which I resolved with Apple just days before I needed the new phone.

I took my lunchtime walk down Second Avenue to Houston Street, then up Third Avenue and back along St. Mark's Place; I almost always listened to music and carried my handbag when I walked down into the Village as part of my routine. This particular day was bright and sunny, but I smelled an autumn musk in the air. There lingered an acrid odor of burning leaves as I walked by the church. I looked carefully around at my surroundings for signs of smoke. I saw a white puff of smoke coming from the ICON construction site. I stopped at the corner opposite the church and tapped a woman on the shoulder.

"Does that look like smoke over there?" I asked her.

"Yes, it does," she said.

"Do you think I should call the police?" I asked.

She paused, then agreed. "Yes, I think so," she said.

I pulled my phone from my bag and dialed 911.

"Nine-one-one operator. What is your emergency?" the woman said.

"Hi, yes, I see white smoke coming from a construction site on Second Ave., and it smells like burning leaves," I said.

"Where exactly are you, ma'am?" the operator asked.

"Let me look," I said, and stared up at the signs on both blocks. "I'm in front of St. Mark's Church. The ICON construction site is between Tenth and Ninth Streets, on Second Ave. I could be wrong—it could just be dust blowing out the window," I said, looking aimlessly away from the site as she talked.

The woman on the corner tapped my shoulder and pointed back to the building as a thick black cloud of smoke started to billow from the building windows.

"Oh, now there's thick black smoke coming from the building. Now, that looks suspicious," I said.

"We're on our way," the operator said. I hung up the phone.

We heard the sirens approaching. The fire engines rounded the corner a block away.

"Wow, do they always come that fast?" the woman asked me.

"I don't know," I said.

"How did you know their number?" the woman asked.

"I called 911, the emergency number here," I said. *This woman must not be from around here*, I thought.

"Oh," she said.

We stood together, watching the fire truck come to a complete stop at the corner. The firemen began to unroll the hoses.

"Well, I think I'm gonna keep going on my walk," I said. "After all this excitement, I need to walk." I smiled and waved goodbye. I called Chloe to tell her the story while I continued my walk. I needed to talk to my sister. I felt scared and was worried I was being set up.

"I'm scared," I said as soon as Chloe answered the phone.

"Why, what's goin' on?" she asked.

"I'm on my lunchtime walk, and I just had to call 911. I'm so freaking out right now, Chloe. I just reported a fire. Oh my God, I'm so freakin' scared," I said.

"Slow down—I don't understand. What?" she said.

I started to tear up. I took a deep breath and tried to focus. "I was walking by St. Mark's Church and smelled something burning. So I looked around carefully and saw it. There was smoke coming from the ICON construction site. So I stopped and asked a lady on the corner if I should call the police. She said yes, so I did," I said.

"Wow, really? That just happened? Are you sure?" she asked.

"Yes, this is real," I said.

"I'm sorry to have to ask. It's just, after last year, with the hacking and everything, sometimes I don't know when I'm not there with you," she said.

"I swear it really happened," I said.

"So, did the police come?" she asked.

"No, but the fire department came. You know in real life they actually wait for the fire truck to stop before they jump out?" I said.

Chloe laughed, but I could manage only a tense face. "This isn't funny. I'm really freaked out," I said.

"I'm sorry. I feel for you," she said.

"Do you think I'm being set up?" I asked.

"No, I think you just are very observant," she said.

"What if I'm framed for arson or something? Oh, I'm freaking out. I can't stop thinking about the missing notebooks," I said.

"Wait, which notebooks?" she asked.

"The large red notebook. The one with my delusions from when I was first hospitalized. It went missing in June 2011. I had written romance in it, talked about the night Jamie was conceived, then explained what I thought happened to me," I said.

"I don't know—I think you probably just misplaced them," she said.

"The last place I saw them was under my desk at work," I said.

"Why did you take them to work?" she asked.

"I was afraid Jack would destroy them in retaliation for my kicking him out of the house last summer," I said.

"Wow, well, don't leave your notebooks at work. Jeez. But I don't think the missing notebooks are related to what just happened," she said.

"What if someone was setting me up? I wrote a letter saying I'd trust whoever helped me get away from Jack," I said.

"You won't be framed for arson—you reported it. You didn't do anything wrong. They should be thankful you were walking by," she said.

"I feel like I'm gonna puke," I said.

"Did you take your medicine today?" she asked.

"Yeah, I remembered," I said.

"You'll be okay. Just take a really long walk and call me later tonight. I love you," she said.

"I love you, too," I said, as the phone clicked off. Music playing through my headphones, I put my phone back in my bag and kept walking.

After walking for a while, I got nervous and headed back to the office. When I got there, I told everyone what had happened on my walk. I feared I'd be framed for arson or tied to the event somehow because I'd made the 911 call. I needed my coworkers to remember that I had been at work in the morning and had just stepped out on my standard hour-long walk for my alibi. Tim, one of the clinical research associates, told me the next day that he and his friends thought I'd probably saved the entire block by calling it in so quickly.

The next morning when I left my house, there was a big red SUV parked in front of the fire hydrant near my apartment building. It said FIRE CHIEF on the outside of the truck. I worried it was for me, but then I reminded myself we lived a block from the Eleventh Street firehouse in Park Slope. It had to be a coincidence; I tried to put it out of my mind and focus on what was real in my life. I had plans with Hugh that night.

I met him outside the Lyceum Theatre, where we were going to see the play *Venus in Furs*. We ordered wine and went to our seats in the second row—close enough that we could see and hear every line.

Afterward, he took me to a restaurant across the street. Once we had kissed goodbye and walked for a ways, I saw my subway line and tried to part.

"I want you to come home with me to my apartment—see my place, have a drink," he said.

"Okay," I replied nervously, as he trapped my hand and guided me down Twenty-Third Street toward his Chelsea apartment.

Hugh unlocked the door to his apartment and turned on the light. "What do you think?" he asked as we walked in.

"It's practical," I said about the studio with simple white walls, a large bed, a sofa, and little else.

"I stay here when I work in the city. I go home to Long Island for my children two nights per week," he said.

He led me into the room and lit the candle swiftly, as I set down my handbag. I looked at him curiously, not sure how these things started. He reached for my hand, and I took his in mine. He pulled me into an embrace, and I responded to him.

When he touched me, I lost all ability to think or to resist him. He dominated me with his assertiveness. I accepted his advances without any defenses. It was a little after midnight, and I needed to work the next day. Hugh and I fooled around multiple times before I decided I needed to leave. I even felt waves of a leisurely orgasm pass over me in response to one of his climaxes.

"Hugh, I didn't pack an overnight bag. I need to go home."

"Next time you will stay," he said.

I leaned back and kissed him leisurely. "I will," I said.

When I got home from spending the evening with Hugh, I wrote about the orgasm during sex with him in my journal. Suddenly, the Grundig radio, which had been silent, turned on. "Glad You Came," by the Wanted, played. The radio creeped me out; I got paranoid that hackers had set me up with Hugh on OkCupid, and that I was being watched. As much as I wanted to deny my paranoia, when the Grundig radio turned on like that, it seemed like a response to my writing. It spoke to me without my touch. Plus, I would never have gone on the date if I hadn't seen the name like Hugh's in that comic book. I worried my fate was being manipulated. But I figured I'd regret it if I didn't do what the pages told me to do.

The next morning, at the corner of Fourteenth Street and Second Avenue, in front of the New York Eye and Ear Infirmary, I saw something happen. I watched the most beautiful woman's purple handbag crossing the street. Then I blinked and saw a flash of black and realized I was tracking a short woman carrying a purple duffel bag. I knew I was tired, but this was a new symptom.

I tried to remember the rest of the prediction from the comic book. It had shown me dating a man and had told me I would go blind. I began to worry that something was wrong with my eyes. I called my sister as soon as I could (I waited till 7:00 a.m. California time) and told Chloe that I had seen the woman disappear. Worse yet, on the train ride into the city, someone had written "666" on the window with a Sharpie. A woman had stood in front of the door, with the number at her forehead, and I had read it through the glass. The Book of Revelations, which my siblings and I had studied as children, said the mark of the beast would appear on people's foreheads and they would disappear.

"Sunny, don't worry about it. It was just some kid thinking it would be funny. It actually *is* funny," Chloe said. But after I got back from my walk and talk with her, I looked up eye doctors. I couldn't forget the comic book's having told me I'd go blind. I needed to get my eyes checked. I called up and took the next available appointment, that day. This was an eye emergency. I left work early, saying I was sick. I'd make up my absence when I was feeling better.

I arrived at a nice office on Second Avenue. I filled out the paperwork and checked almost every condition listed on the history. I was having issues. I shared about my condition, and my concern that something was wrong with my eyes, although I didn't tell the woman about the comic book, because what if this was a cruel joke? It had to be a hoax, right? If my computer had been hacked and someone was trying to influence my future, then who was the fool? Was it the hacker, for trying to persuade me, or me, for falling into a paranoid state when I didn't have enough data to go on? Plus, I really did need the medication. These constant little reminders had succeeded in making me paranoid and afraid.

The doctor came in and examined my eyes. He found nothing seriously wrong with them, and I was relieved. He gave me a new prescription for glasses, some eye allergy drops, and an eye scrub to reduce blurred vision caused by inflamed eyelids.

A few days later, when I went on my walk, I noticed three NYPD vehicles. The IF YOU SEE SOMETHING, SAY SOMETHING slogan was displayed on the message boards on top of the three cop cars. They drove slowly in front of me for a block. I needed a cigarette. I decided to stop and buy a pack. I'd relapsed during my divorce and my struggle to deal with my return to medication; lighting up helped me to cope. Cigarettes eased the side effects of my psychiatric medications and improved my perception of my thinking and concentration.

The three cars pulled over on the right side of the road. When I came out, they were still there. For another two blocks, they slowly cruised and stopped. I kept walking, stopping only to light a cigarette. Things kept happening that I didn't understand, and I kept feeling reluctant to say anything.

When I got back to my office after my walk at lunch, I sat at my desk and unlocked the desk drawers on the left. When the drawer opened, my pulse picked up. My papers. Someone had returned some of my missing papers. The minutes from the health care association I volunteered with, and the association financials, had come back. They'd gone missing the previous summer from my red briefcase.

Everyone had told me not to worry about it. "Sunny, you just misplaced them," Erik had told me.

I had let go of my anxiety about the missing documents, but amid the fire department tailing me and the messages from the NYPD squad cars, it returned. The reappearance of some of these papers made me worry about the notebooks that were still missing, especially the large red notebook in which I had written my deepest-seated concerns from my pregnancy. There was too much I couldn't explain, and this was the final straw. I had to say something. This was real.

If you see something, say something. The police cars' signs had told me I needed to say something.

I pressed the COMPOSE button in my Gmail account and started typing. "I am going against my parents' and friends' advice by sharing this, but lately things have been happening to me that scare me. I'm telling you this because when things happen that I can't explain, I always ask for advice from someone else, especially someone whom I can trust. I need advice. I'm sorry I waited so long. It is just that I am afraid now. I'm trusting that you will know how best to handle this situation. . . . "

I shared everything. I needed another perspective. I wasn't sure how the e-mail would be received. I wanted somebody to tell me what was going on. I needed confirmation or, conversely, to be discredited. But the only way to do that was through sharing and by gaining insight from someone who had power and knowledge. I figured going back to the beginning was the only way anybody would understand my story.

I sent the message to the person with the greatest authority, knowledge, and power at work: Dan. I disclosed my mental health condition, alluding to the writing from when I was sick that could be harmful to him, because my issue focused on him.

That night I waited up, hoping I'd hear back from Dan before work the next day. A little after 11:00 p.m., his message came. He apologized for being behind on e-mail and respectfully suggested I consult with my doctor, to be on the safe side, but also recommended that I contact someone in HR who was very discreet and would help with my theft issues.

I woke up, climbed out of bed, and started my routine. When I got to the kitchen to start the coffee, I stopped at the kitchen table to unlock the screen on my laptop. That's when I noticed a single playing card faceup on the table: the ace of spades. I knew it couldn't have been Jamie who'd left it, because she was at her dad's house. Jack and I had been separated for almost a year now, and I was slowly readying myself to file for divorce. Even facing possible unemployment, I couldn't imagine staying married to him.

A few minutes later, Sophie came in. "Hey, Sophie, any chance you were playing cards last night?" I asked.

"No, why?" she asked, still half-asleep and in need of nourishment.

"Well, this morning I saw this on the table, and I don't remember it being there last night," I said.

"Ha," she laughed.

"Why is that funny?" I asked.

"It's the sign of the joker," she said.

"Oh," I said, and did an online search for "sign of the joker." I couldn't find what Sophie was talking about, but it bothered me sufficiently to play over in the back of my mind. The only explanation was that I had been sleepwalking, Sophie had been sleepwalking, or someone was stalking us. I didn't like any of these options. Worst-case scenario, hackers had found access to pharmacy records and were stalking mentally ill people. A few weeks later, when a shooting at a movie theater in Colorado occurred, I was unsettled by the memory of having seen the sign of the joker in my home.

Following the instructions from Dan, I e-mailed HR to set up an appointment. When I arrived at HR, I was interviewed by a nice, midcareer HR representative. The woman took notes, as I shared the significance of the missing documents.

"A notebook went missing that had directions to the Lanier copier that would give access to any documents that were imaged in the department. Also, other items that had gone missing were financial documents from the health care association I volunteered with. Those were the items that concerned me most; the rest were personal documents that went missing," I said. I did not elaborate with the woman. She handed me a few documents about resources for wellness.

After I reported the theft issue, I wanted to finish the process I'd started with Jack. Dating had liberated me from his degrading view. Men were telling me they wanted me for the first time in years. I felt the weight of Jack's silent oppression lifted. I was freed, and I knew I could never be with Jack again.

It was the end of May when I set up the appointment. We met at the lawyer's office to sign all the divorce paperwork. We passed the pages around the table and signed each copy as an original. The agreement was generous for the first three years, then standard.

One day in late August, the news said a blue moon would be out that night. I went to open my mail and got the letter from my lawyer. The divorce was final. I got on the phone and called everyone.

"It feels good getting a divorce, once in a blue moon," I said. My friends and family laughed at the coincidence. It felt right. I was happy to have a new beginning.

I kept seeing Hugh. We'd meet for lunch at his place in Chelsea. It was a romance unlike any I'd ever had before. I told him everything, and he started to mark me. He became part of me, as I wrote for him.

But our relationship was not simple. We each had our own children and career, and Hugh had other women. I tried not to mind, but every few months I broke up with him to try dating, only to find I wanted to seek refuge in his embrace. When it got too complicated for me, I finally broke up with him and continued to live my own life.

As I sat at my desk one afternoon in January after I sent Hugh an e-mail telling him I wanted to be his again, Gmail went down for an hour or so, and Twitter started to fill up quickly with anxious tweets in response. I knew something was wrong when an important e-mail delivery to me was delayed twenty minutes. I sat at my computer the whole time, but there was a time stamp on a message from Jamie's principal at school that was off by twenty minutes. The e-mail said my daughter's school had gone into a soft lockdown because an unidentified person was in the building. Terrified, I went on Twitter to see what happened; when I saw someone else notice anomalies in his Gmail, I searched for "Gmail" tweets. My browser printed my early search for "Gmail," but I hadn't given the print command; the computer was acting independent of me.

The early tweets were filled with tension, worry, and panic. Then I refreshed to update my "Gmail" search. Tweets were suppressed. The early tweets of panic were missing. Instead, funny tweets remained. I rebooted my browser and checked my virus definitions, and everything seemed fine.

The e-mail from my daughter's school said everything was okay. The soft lockdown had lasted only fifteen minutes. I sat at my computer, contemplating our world and the future. I felt little hope. My guiding light, my hope for love, was flickering and growing dim inside me.

Tossing and turning in my bed that night, I came to a new conclusion. What made me better was hope for the future. Everybody needs that. The thought of seeing my daughter grow up into a strong and independent woman, someday holding my grandchildren, and being the mother I wanted to be called out to me. The problem was my priorities. My awakening had captivated my every brain cell. To put it to bed and get back to my life, I needed to finish what I had set out to do. I needed to explain what had happened to me. Writing is an inherently political process, and one of the reasons I had to write my story was to have a sort of life insurance policy.

My mom said I should just let all this go: "The details don't matter anymore. Just accept it happened and move on."

I considered taking her advice. But I couldn't let it go, because I didn't feel safe doing so. I remembered the missing notebooks. I remembered the fires. Letting it go was possibly more dangerous than connecting the dots and trying to find the truth about what happened to me.

I trusted the people around me to guide me when I was not well. I trusted the people who loved me in real life (possibly naively) to follow the golden rule: treat others the way you wish to be treated. Plus, if I was being targeted, what was to say this wouldn't happen to others? Would others stay sane? All those constant reminders? Was I sick because of my genetics, or did my environment trigger me? What I did know was that I must trust the people around me whom I loved. Without trust and love, my life had no meaning. I knew enough to understand that psychopaths and those hungry for power misused trust, but I refused to believe our society should live in fear of them. Why had the IMPORTANT MESSAGE note appeared on my desk right when I received the message alerting me that something was wrong with my SIM card, and just before the big fire in the East Village? I hoped someone was watching over me.

I met Hugh for lunch in February. We saw each other another two times after that, and each time I felt closer to him, but my vision of my future kept getting darker.

"Remember, I've known you two hundred years," he said, as he pinned me against his bed and looked deeply into me. "I own your body, mind, and soul. Remember that," he demanded.

I'd been seeing Hugh off and on for two years. He was Hindu, Brahman, a member of the highest priest class. I loved him but wondered why he believed we'd known each other so long. He said something about the dreams he was having. I worried about him.

I had also started to contemplate my relationship with men in general. By seeking superficial needs and dating freely, I was never going to get my deeper needs met. I struggled between my delusional hope for the physician's love, my concern that I had been artificially manipulated and given false hope about the physician's love, and the idea that I desired a mythical relationship. I struggled between a hope for a future where I could be loved like I felt in my delusions of Dr. Richard, and the stark reality of needing to love myself and build loving connections in my real life.

"See"

Concerned about the possibility of my browser turning on me, isolating me from reality, and telling me to do things, I decided I needed to talk about it more.

"Erik, I want to think of who had something to gain from my losing touch," I said as we sat on my stoop one evening in March after Jamie was asleep.

"Are you sure you need to do that?" he asked, worried about my focus returning to my issue.

I paused to take a swig from my bottle of Brooklyn Lager. "I mean, did you hear that NPR show earlier this week that was e-mailed around? It says the prison system is the new institution for people with mental illness," I said, looking down at the sidewalk, reflecting on how I could end up like anyone else.

"You know the weight of the world does not belong on your shoulders," Erik said.

"But if I don't say anything, if I just stay quiet about what happened, how many others will be susceptible to getting hacked?"

"But you were so sick. How do you know it wasn't just part of the illness?" he asked seriously.

I pulled out a cigarette from my small change purse and lit it. "The more time away from it, the more I can see," I said, exhaling a plume of smoke. "When I take the medication, I can think through it." I paused, then looked over at Erik. "Did I tell you about the letter I wrote in the fall?" I asked.

"I don't think so," he said.

"Well, I wrote to Medicaid's expansion committee and argued

my case is less expensive to treat than if I were institutionalized. The argument was strong," I said, tossing the half-smoked cigarette into the street. "The first time a person is triggered and set off into psychosis is the most difficult to navigate. They don't often know how to ground themselves in trusted relationships. But after everything I've been through, I have a system for dealing, and I've learned how to cope when my unwanted triggers push me into insanity."

"But what if you are just different?" Erik asked.

The concept of people with mental illness being identified, tracked, and agitated sufficiently to act out was possible, but I didn't think Erik liked to believe it. It raised the hairs on the back of my neck to consider what it would be like to be messaged without the solid embrace of my support team, and without medication to help me deal with my fear of my technology acting up.

"Erik, there *is* stuff going on. You know that Twitter is being filtered and censored, right?" I said.

"What does it matter?" he asked.

"My machine tried to print a search for 'Gmail' tweets, before the Twitter suppression started for the Gmail outage," I said.

"Really?" he asked.

"Yeah, I knew about the outage because Jamie's school had an unidentified man in the school and they went into a soft lockdown. The principal sent out an e-mail to the parents. I was sitting at my computer at the time the notification went out, but the time stamp on the e-mail didn't match the delivery time; there was a delay. Because of my hypervigilance, I checked to see what was going on in the world, to be certain all was well. That's when I noticed the first tweets about the Gmail outage. I searched before the tweet suppression started regarding Gmail tweets. Then the printer printed the search," I said.

"That *is* weird," Erik said.

There were lots of possible forces involved. My secrets were not actually that big. My Myspace account had revealed my secret messages to the physician all the way back in 2006. Eight years had passed since then—lots of time for that secret to be sold. I'd even e-mailed the major pharmaceutical companies, sharing that they needed more stories like mine to give hope to those taking their medications.

Another one of my ideas involved people who had been targeted to become ill and carry out attacks against the public. I thought it was possible to develop immunity to later targeting, through developing coping skills, and I believed I exemplified the way some targeted individuals learned from the experience. I learned how to cope. I stayed grounded in the people around me. Taking only what I wanted from the constant little reminders and messages, I kept it real, on more than one occasion.

Granted, I showed my paranoia for a few days after the issue with my computer trying to show me the Twitter suppression, by printing my search for "Gmail" during the outage. As I read about NSA components, I remembered how my computer had acted in 2011. I also considered who had the power to manipulate me. My first thought was that Republicans were to blame for my being targeted to foil Dr. Richard's chances of success. Then I suspected Democrats in power could also be destroying young politicians, trying to poison the well of the younger generation. Or it could be the Tea Party—they were just fringe enough to want to unravel the threads of modern civilization by violating the unspoken rules of Internet ethics. Unsure of whom I could trust, I made copies of all my files and documented everything.

I sat editing my manuscript when the last message came. When I started scrolling up, my computer took on a life of its own. It scrolled a hundred pages to find the sentence "I wanted pregnancy to be fun."

Then I touched the keypad, trying to unhighlight the passage. It jumped forward several pages and highlighted the single word "see"—as if the file were commanding me to have greater vision.

I suddenly worried about Jamie. Where was she? I heard a commotion in the hallway. A worker was removing a lamp in preparation for our move away from Park Slope and its steep rents. We were moving to a nice building in a new neighborhood.

The power tool buzzed in the hall, and the door was wide open. Our newly adopted dog, Buddy, had suddenly stopped barking. Jamie had put him on a leash to guide him into the hallway, to help him not be so afraid.

I looked down the staircase to see her. "Jamie?" I asked.

"I'm just showing Buddy there's nothing to be afraid of," she said. The worker's tools were spread about the floor, and Buddy quieted immediately once he was able to see the source of the noise.

I stopped working on the manuscript and spent the rest of the afternoon packing with Jamie and Buddy. As I loaded the boxes and packed up our things, I started to plan. Grounded through relationships and writing, I understood that the only way to light up my future was to protect my voice, write, and tell my story. I wanted my voice to be heard.

I needed to mend. I wanted to be the mother I had envisioned myself being before the birth. I needed to tell my story, forgive, and let it go. I had missed so much of motherhood wrapped up in the memories, illness, and experiences of it all that I was missing the most important part of my relationship with my future: my connection with my daughter. I needed to learn to be with her, not locked up in my mind. I needed to connect as a mother. She needed me—she always had.

When Jamie and I next talked that evening, she told me exactly what she thought. "It's immature of you to work on your book and ignore me so much," she told me.

"I hope that someday you'll understand how sick I was, and how I needed to make sense of things. I hope you'll forgive me one day."

Later that night, my thoughts turned toward Dr. Richard, as they usually did when I was having a bad day. At first I enjoyed thinking of him, but then I became overwhelmed by the idea that he was trying to hurt me. Devastated, frozen, panicked, anxious, afraid, sad— every feeling I'd ever had came rolling over me at once, as I recalled his anger toward me for having wanted him so badly. His writing to me that my e-mails were inappropriate, and the correspondence from the Roundtable Associates, still kept me in check. But who had hacked me, if he in fact had not? I still wanted it to be Dr. Richard who had hacked me, because I wanted him to love me like that, but I also wanted to have permission to be angry at whoever had done it. I mean, who did they think they were, God? Nobody should be interfered with and tinkered with the way I had, without consent. I was processing my repressed anger for the first time. I'd been through despair when confronted with reality—now I was angry.

I knew the only way I'd be able to let go of these feelings and move on was if I felt this way. Still, I wrestled with the memory of loving Dr. Richard. The idea was so deeply rooted in me, so much a part of me, that I didn't know how to release the roots and repot it somewhere else besides my heart. I'd watered it with so many tears and years of growth that it had matured.

What I thought might be effective would be to date until I found someone whom I wanted enough to feel again. I thought back to a conversation I'd had with Dr. Mitchel, who had recently asked me if I was in love again when I'd told him about my relationship with Hugh.

"Well, you know, there are a lot of fish in the sea. Eventually I'm bound to find a good one, but for now it's catch and release. Maybe someday I'll reel in a keeper," I said, uncommitted to the idea. He laughed really hard.

What I failed to say was, *I'm still in love with the memory of Dr. Richard, and until I stop loving him, I don't know that I'll fully engage with another man. I mean, how can I totally love someone when part of my heart belongs to someone who doesn't want me?* I hated seeing my problem written simply on paper. It made me cringe; honesty tends to do that when you confront a delusional belief. But I didn't want to be delusional. I wanted realness. Still, how could I not love him? It hurt my soul.

I shook my head and resigned myself to hold on to hope but try to release him. Although I was shining professionally, my hope for Dr. Richard's love darkened and was eventually replaced by real love from friends and family.

As a member of a writing team with other researchers and statisticians to oversee the numbers, I coauthored peer-reviewed scientific literature. I took the writing skills I learned to stay grounded personally and applied them professionally. Professional connections began to think of me to write articles for their publications, and I started being published in some of my areas of interest. I was also invited to participate in leadership at volunteer organizations.

In October 2014, I attended a conference in Washington, DC. It was inspirational to hear personal stories from others in the profession who were living with chronic illness—mostly cancer, tumors, depression, joint disorders, and stories of loss. At the opening session, the group discussed professional identity, and I kept thinking about my story and how sharing it would go. I was struck by how as human beings we must accept ourselves as individuals and see our strengths before we move forward as professionals.

When I talked with one of the presenters at the conference and shared my story, I asked for insight. I wanted to know whether it would harm me or my affiliations to publish my story. I hung on to her words when she told me to publish.

"Get over it, and move on," she said to me gently. The weight of her silence hung heavily at the end of the sentence. I was tired of holding my story inside, so I decided to take her advice. I trusted her. I mean, what was the worst that could happen?

Epilogue

My belief in Dr. Richard's love guided me as I learned to cope with madness. We both lived in this universe. Sometimes in my fantasy world we did specific activities, like bowling; other times we just stood there near each other. I still get tears if I think about it too much.

I lost so many years trying to come to terms with my awakening. I felt the loss of my vision of a family the way I set out to have it. But I have hope that someday Jamie will forgive me for the times I failed as a mother and for the time I spent writing my story in an attempt to find a way forward, out of the past. To move on, I needed to make sense of what happened to me.

I'm taking a path forward by building a massive network of professional connections, family, friends, and trusted others who sustain me and give me a new type of hope for my future. I've decided I don't want a single relationship to fill the void in my life that Jack left after my twenties and early thirties. I still spend time with Sophie and stay in touch with Ava. Hugh and I occasionally connect, but I'm hopeful for a man I can envision happiness with. Someone to be with some of the time. A comfortable addition to my life, not the focus of it. On my good days, I've given up on romantic love. On the bad days, well, thankfully, they don't last all day long. Mostly they just pass in short stretches. I am avoiding my triggers, and I'm slowly healing through positive connections with the people around me who listen.

When I reflect on how I feel about Dr. Richard, I recognize that he will never love me. I listened to my friends, family, and loved ones when they explained it to me over and over again. But deep inside, part of me wants him, or the memory of who I thought he was. I haven't been able to forget how I felt. Maybe if I could have known him, reality would have taught me. As it is, I have this deep hope that someday he could change his mind and love me, but then my friends and family actively work to deplete that hope, which was a protective delusion through my struggle to know real from not real. I suppose if he had treated me the way David Letterman treated his stalker, who suffered from erotomanic delusions, I could have ended up like her: dead. But I had something special: I was allowed to maintain hope, and the Roundtable Associates set a clear boundary for me. I took very seriously their threat to sue me. Even though most people believe delusions are wrong, for me, loving Dr. Richard was a protective force.

What I have learned is that if I go back into the memory as who I've become, respecting the changes I've undergone to cope with my story, I am better able to see myself as transformed and feel less disabled by the memory. I struggle when I remember myself in that magical moment where I was changing without reflecting on myself today. For instance, when I think of my labor, if I can be there as if I'm traveling with the ghost of Christmas past, I am able to see the story for what it was. I was a woman touched at the most vulnerable time in her life in a sort of God-and-science moment, and my brain broke in response to my physiological transformation. Jamie's birth set off a sequence of changes in thought that led to my departure from reality because of a dysfunctional brain disease. It was too much for me to recognize as I was enduring it, but I learned to cope with my flawed memory bank.

What I needed while I was enduring it was treatment without side effects, real hope, real love, and honest insight. I needed to tell my story and have people listen to it. It took me years to learn how to tell my story, and it took even longer to teach people how I want them to respond. I want them to thank me for trusting them and focus their attention on my strengths, not my weaknesses. I work actively to transform the listener through my telling of what I want and need. I give them insight into how to respond while they listen.

The one thing I didn't really have when I was recovering was lots of stories and role models for this listening exchange. I felt like I was forging new ground. But I had everything else: privilege, education, stability, support, and work. I'd heard this rumbling about recovery, but it was faint and distant and there were few public stories of success. I would have liked to have read a story like mine. It would have meant so much to me to read something by someone who was able to make sense of her story and then turn it into a meaningful narrative.

Losing touch with reality and realizing morality is relative was soul crushing to me. By that, I mean that when I was in the hospital and felt coerced into following the signs, and then the medication brought me back to reality, it was harsh. I realized I was ready to follow the signs and disobey the social norms and ethics I was raised to abide because of the perversion of psychosis. It broke my heart that I could have been criminalized. But I was lucky. I had access to appropriate care. I was in a safe place when I lost touch. I was treated in a hospital psychiatric care unit and given medication that was effective for me. It wasn't as if I came from a low socioeconomic status and didn't have access to services or was taken in by the criminal justice system as my only method to access care.

I will say that when Ellen Saks shared her story in her book *The Center Cannot Hold*, I found the first real hope and inspiration I could hold on to. She didn't share much delusional content, just the idea that she understood on a similar level what I experienced, and the idea that she was smart, worked full-time, and produced good writing amazed me and made me view her as a role model.

These days, my symptoms are rare. My daily medication routine is effective, and my writing speaks for itself. I am not a threat to myself or others. I hope people will see my strengths as I navigated illness to live my life with effective care.

In the fall of 2014, when I started seeing a new psychiatrist, my diagnosis was reclassified as schizophrenia. That was hard to hear. I think they did me a favor by delaying the diagnosis. Don't get me wrong—I was treated immediately and effectively for delusional disorder and psychosis, using the same medication they use to treat schizophrenia, so the correct diagnosis didn't impact my finding the right medication. Because I was treated effectively, I believe my mind was allowed to recover more quickly than it would have if treatment had been delayed.

For me, the diagnosis is more a description of symptoms or "outcomes" than a helpful tool. Having a label sucks. While I identify with my mental experience as core to who I am, and embrace my life, getting the diagnosis code 295.3 written on my bill was not a helpful event for me. It made me sad. I'd be fine with knowing I have a general cluster of misunderstood symptoms in the 295.3 range, but the health care community should acknowledge that the exact type of brain disease I have is still misunderstood. It isn't like they did a blood test or looked for the cause in my DNA. Even the National Institutes of Health realized diagnostic terminology was outdated and their study methods were wasteful.

Studying social behavior in people with a biologically based mental illness is like trying to study the use of facial tissues in people with allergies. It misses the point. I didn't actually need a definitive diagnosis to know that I needed treatment. Taking medications immediately (trying half the atypical antipsychotics on the market to find the right fit) was not impeded by my lack of a firm diagnosis or of insurance preauthorization.

My schizophrenia diagnosis took almost a decade to confirm. During that time, I grew as a person and learned that I am not a diagnosis. Diagnosis is something that some people surrender to or are defeated by because therapy does not exist to treat it adequately. Granted, a lot of people need an explanation when they lose their mind. Associations like the American Psychiatric Association, in an attempt to apply their authority by using a label for people who suffer certain symptoms (like delusions and hallucinations), probably didn't realize the potential unintended consequences of labeling people when they created diagnostic criteria for madness. I vote they call it "madness of unknown origin," explain it may be a disease they don't yet know, and say they are going to try therapies that are not fully understood, hoping for a cure. Instead, in its attempt to categorize and classify without a solid understanding of the disease process, the APA threw away generations of people who experience mental illness. People's lives are impacted by these false systems of labeling. People are marginalized because of madness, and society has accepted these flawed labels for madness, rather than searching for the cause and finding the cure.

I am thankful my medical team delayed my diagnosis of severe mental illness for years. That gave me time to grow and emotionally prepare to deal with the challenges of stigma and the discrimination that occurs as a result of labeling.

A diagnosis of severe mental illness is very broad, and lots of different conditions are currently being called the same thing. In the book *Brain on Fire*, the author, Susannah Cahalan, is treated for an autoimmune condition that causes severe behavioral changes when it attacks her brain. Her illness is first classified as mental illness, but, through her family's refusal to accept traditional approaches to care, she receives an innovative treatment at NYU's research-based medical center. She recovers fully after treatment with a novel therapy that improves her immune functioning. When I read her story, I had a new appreciation for how greatly we misunderstand brain disease.

While "diagnosis" using our flawed system of terminology takes time, I found that learning coping skills was essential to living with symptoms of madness and having a meaningful life. I'm not saying that I'd go it alone without some form of treatment. For me, when I take my medication, my symptoms are few and far between. But during the times when I've missed doses and have had breakthrough thoughts, knowing how to ground my thoughts has been helpful. Learning skills like writing, focusing on protective concepts, and applying semantics helped me while my medication had yet to take hold.

I believed I communicated with an unknown force during psychosis when I was taken off medication (2006 and 2011), and I documented everything. But trusting the people around me was my greatest strength. Friends and family helped me see how drastically I had misunderstood my circumstances at that time. I gained insight through trusting the people around me, and writing helped me to ground my thoughts once the medication brought my mind back to reality. Today, effective strategies are known that help build trust in relationships. My favorite method is called LEAP®. It was developed by Dr. Xavier Amador. Chloe started to use this after attending training at a NAMI family-to-family course. The training program transforms relationships and teaches skills to build trust in relationships.

"It is easier to support you knowing how to help," Chloe said as she drove home from her last class in February 2015. I'd called concerned about something.

"Yeah, I save all the best calls for you," I said, half kidding, half serious.

"I don't think mom realizes the level of difficulty of some of these calls. I'm thousands of miles away, and I'm supposed to know what is real?" Chloe asked. "I mean, it's hard."

"You've done a great job. Your support means so much to me. Even if you didn't know what to say, your heart has always been there for me, and just being on the phone with me is what matters," I said.

As part of my journey to healing and telling my story, I started to heal my soul. My decision to begin to "disclose" over the years to countless people in my personal and professional life has brought tremendous relief, but stigmatization is real. I've had people turn their backs, ignore me, or do worse after my disclosure. I believe that these people who shunned and stigmatized me did so because they were not aware of the biological basis of this disease. Their unfamiliarity made them afraid because they couldn't see me as a person. They saw me only as having a stereotypical label, and associated my diagnosis with "behaviors."

At this point in my journey, I am okay with my story and feel that if others can't handle it, then that is their issue. I no longer value myself based on responses from strangers. It took a long time to learn that. I realize that individuals are able to accept things based only on where they are in their journey through life.

I live a full life writing, mothering my daughter, and caring for our family dog. I understand that friends, family, and other people who love me will meet my deeper needs. Everyone's love has contributed to my ability to return to my mainstream work and advance in my career. All I needed to have was the opportunity to prove my ability, and work that I find interesting. Community support has made reality a place I want to stay. I'm grateful for being sustained in little ways, like by all the people who listen.

I have forgiven my mind for breaking like it did, but letting go of false memories has been the hardest part of my journey. I trust the people around me who've told me that my perception of Dr. Richard was wrong. Through trusting the people around me, I'm letting go. I've released Dr. Richard from my mind. I'm not promising I'll be perfect at this, but I'm trying to move on. I love my life and look forward to watching my beautiful daughter grow up to be a strong and independent woman. I trust that if I start to fall off the ladder again, others will pick me back up and put me back on.

Acknowledgments

When I've told people my story in person, most have been supportive, and I feel real love through having shared. The professional connections I've told have had the greatest impact on me.

I'd like to thank my family, for always being there for me on the other end of the phone or Skype connection, and all my friends who have listened to me again and again, and many more who have vocalized support. Most of the men from OkCupid, and even random strangers, who took time to chat with me were considerate.

I'd like to thank Swenson Book Development for its tremendous input in the early days of writing, and for helping me find She Writes Press.

I learned so much from Gotham Writers' Workshop and my many wonderful classmates who shared their stories. I'd like to thank Writer's Digest for their courses, too.

The book would not be what it is today without She Writes Press and Annie Tucker.

Special thanks to my medical providers for giving me the appropriate care when I needed it.

Thank you to the moderators at Psychforums. Your near-limitless caring has made a huge difference in my life. Having a virtual community has been a source of wonderful healing and peer support. Also, thank you to NAMI for providing community support. I recommend that everyone join #IWillListen.

Professionally, I'd like to thank my associations for always accepting me. And I would like to thank the many mentors who have shaped and influenced my career.

About the Author

I'm a mother who writes and lives in Brooklyn, New York, where I landed by way of New Hampshire. I was inspired to write the book *All in Her Head: A Novel* after my diagnosis of severe mental illness and my battle with postpartum depression, psychosis, and delusional disorder.

I come from a privileged, educated, and stable home; I grew up attending a small, private Christian school that my parents and their friends founded in our attic in Topeka, Kansas. Thankfully, medication is effective for me and I wasn't criminalized for my illness. On my journey, the thing I needed was more role models to explain how to share. I needed to hear stories of people who told their stories, and see more stories explaining how to teach others to listen. This would have helped so much during my dark days and then during my early days of insight. I've spent the last decade writing a narrative I can live with. Now that I'm finished with this story, I can work on what I want: mothering and writing about things that aren't centered on me. I'm sharing this story with the aspiration that others will share my real hope for building a reality that is a place we want to live.

SELECTED TITLES FROM SHE WRITES PRESS

She Writes Press is an independent publishing company
founded to serve women writers everywhere.
Visit us at www.shewritespress.com.

Insatiable: A Memoir of Love Addiction by Shary Hauer
$16.95, 978-1-63152-982-5
An intimate and illuminating account of corporate executive—and secret
love addict—Shary Hauer's migration from destructive to healthy love.

Fire Season: A Memoir by Hollye Dexter
$16.95, 978-1-63152-974-0
After she loses everything in a fire, Hollye Dexter's life spirals downward
and she begins to unravel—but when she finds herself at the brink of
losing her husband, she is forced to dig within herself for the strength to
keep her family together.

Learning to Eat Along the Way by Margaret Bendet
$16.95, 978-1-63152-997-9
After interviewing an Indian holy man, newspaper reporter Margaret
Bendet follows him in pursuit of enlightenment and ends up facing
demons that were inside her all along.

A Different Kind of Same: A Memoir by Kelley Clink
$16.95, 978-1-63152-999-3
Several years before Kelley Clink's brother hanged himself, she
attempted suicide by overdose. In the aftermath of his death, she traces
the evolution of both their illnesses, and wonders: If he couldn't make it,
what hope is there for her?

Seeing Red: A Woman's Quest for Truth, Power, and the Sacred by
Lone Morch $16.95, 978-1-938314-12-4
One woman's journey over inner and outer mountains—a quest that
takes her to the holy Mt. Kailas in Tibet, through a seven-year marriage,
and into the arms of the fierce goddess Kali, where she discovers her
powerful, feminine self.

*Mothering Through the Darkness: Women Open Up About the
Postpartum Experience* edited by Stephanie Sprenger and Jessica
Smock $16.95, 978-1-63152-804-0
A collection of thirty powerful essays aimed at spreading awareness
and dispelling myths about postpartum depression and perinatal mood
disorders.